THE RELENTLESS PURSUIT OF THE TRUTH

A Tribute to Jacqueline Jane Wurst,
Hospital Corpsman 2nd Class,
United States Navy

Thomas E. Brannon, Special Agent, NCIS, Retired

authorHOUSE®

AuthorHouse™
1663 Liberty Drive, Suite 200
Bloomington, IN 47403
www.authorhouse.com
Phone: 1-800-839-8640

*This book is a work of non-fiction. Unless otherwise noted, the author
and the publisher make no explicit guarantees as to the accuracy of
the information contained in this book and in some cases, names of
people and places have been altered to protect their privacy.*

First published by AuthorHouse 9/12/2007

ISBN: 978-1-4343-2812-0 (sc)
ISBN: 978-1-4343-2813-7 (hc)

Library of Congress Control Number: 2007906068

Printed in the United States of America
Bloomington, Indiana

This book is printed on acid-free paper.

ACRONYMS

AD2	Aviation Mechanic, U.S. Navy Rate
BEQ	Bachelor Enlisted Quarters, U.S. Navy
CDR	Commander, U.S. Navy Rank
CO	Commanding Officer
ER	Hospital Emergency Room
FOIA	Freedom of Information Act
GCM	General Courts Martial
HM1	Hospital Corpsman, U.S. Navy Rate
HM2	Hospital Corpsman, U.S. Navy Rate
ICU	Intensive Care Unit
JAG	Judge Advocate General
KCSO	Kings County Sheriff's Office
LVN	Licensed Vocational Nurse
MD	Medical Doctor
MIA	Missing in Action
MSC	Medical Service Corp, U.S. Navy
NAS	Naval Air Station
NCIS	Naval Criminal Investigative Service
NIS	Naval Investigative Service
ONI	Office of Naval Intelligence, U.S. Navy
POW	Prisoner of War
RN	Registered Nurse

SRB	Military Service Record Book, U.S. Navy
USN	United States Navy
USS	Untied States Ship
WWll	World War ll
YN2	Yeoman 2nd Class, U.S. Navy Rate
187PC	Homicide, California Penal Code
190.2a	Death Penalty or life imprisonment without parole special circumstances, California Penal Code
211PC	Robbery, California Penal Code
261a	Rape, California Penal Code

To Donald and Phyllis Wurst

TABLE OF CONTENTS

PROLOGUE

Tom Brannon served twenty-eight years as a Special Agent with the Naval Criminal Investigative Service, now known to everyone by the acronym NCIS. The current TV series by that name has taught the world about an organization that previously was unknown to most individuals, unless you were a military person and especially if you were a Navy or Marine Corps person in trouble. During Tom's long career which included the Vietnam era he worked many different types of crimes from petty thefts to homicides, from stealing military secrets to spy cases. He had been trained with a specialty of Polygraph Examiner, a sometimes controversial subject, but one which he was known for as being the "best in the business" by all his contemporaries. He was well known for being very objective in his dealings with individuals requiring or requesting a polygraph to determine the truth regarding an issue.

His ability to communicate and establish rapport with people on any level was one of his greatest assets in conducting the thousands of interviews he was involved in during those decades. Ask him and he will even tell you of the time he was traveling through a major airport and felt a large hand on his shoulder. He turned around and a large man with a big smile on his face said, "Hi, I just got out of prison and I remember you". The man was one of his subjects he had polygraphed and it was determined he was involved in a homicide and he then confessed to Tom. The man was guilty and had served his time in prison, but there was no animosity towards Tom as he had been totally fair in his dealings with the individual.

Tom has many stories to tell but the one which haunted him all these years is this one. He has told it over and over to all who would listen. Tom never met Jackie Wurst that he is aware of. They were both stationed together in Japan at the same time and perhaps their paths crossed at the Naval Hospital at some point. But their backgrounds were similar, their duty stations the same, and they both had that same desire to help those around them. They both took their respective professions seriously and conducted themselves in the most professional way possible.

When Tom became involved in Jackie's case he felt such a determination to find her killer to bring justice to Jackie and her family. As the case became colder and colder he was still constantly on the lookout for information to solve this crime. At the request of various NCIS offices he conducted interviews and polygraphs throughout the western United States, all of which cleared those subjects of any involvement in Jackie's case. More than once when he was talking about the unsolved murder he was told, "Why do you care? It's over a long time ago. Why don't you just forget it?" But you don't tell that to Tom Brannon. His RELENTLESS PURSUIT OF THE TRUTH propels him on and this is that story.

Bev Brannon

CHAPTER 1

IT BEGAN AS A ROUTINE DAY—

That Sunday at the Lemoore Naval Air Station Hospital, located in the San Joaquin Valley of central California, began as just a routine day. HM1 Harvey Wade Dwyer, known to everyone as OJ, was the leading Petty Officer in charge of the clinic and he had plenty of paper work which had to be finished. He needed to review and prep his squadron's health records for an upcoming major inspection. Plenty of work to be done and not much time for anything else that day. It was a beautiful day, October 5, 1980-----clear, not too hot but still warm for the time of year.

Jackie Wurst, a young hospital corpsman, arrived at the hospital at 11:00 AM to collect meal fees in the mess hall for the noon meal. This was just a little extra job she had in addition to her regular medical duties. Afterwards, she and OJ had lunch together and talked until about 12:30 when they both needed to get on with their day's schedules. Jackie and OJ walked to the ER section of the hospital, they hugged as friends often do, and she walked through the big ER doors, turned and waved, smiled her famous grin and was on her way.

Jackie had a four-hour break before she had to report back to work, and was going off to ride her bike and then study for promotion exams which would be held soon. She and OJ had spent most of the lunch time talking about those exams and she was concerned she wouldn't pass high enough to advance in rank. OJ assured her that if he could pass she certainly could as he felt in comparison he had a "slow brain". He knew she was sharp and quick and he knew for sure she would pass easily.

About 4:45 in the afternoon, the Chief of the Day asked OJ if he knew where Jackie was as she was late for checking in for the evening meal collection. Jackie was never late. A sudden weird feeling was in the pit of OJ's stomach and he went out to drive around the base looking for her. By 6:30 a check with her friends and co-workers revealed she had not been seen or heard from since leaving on her break about 12:30. A phone call to the local Police Department was unproductive since departmental policy at the time required a person to be missing for twenty-four hours before police could become involved and initiate a search. Concern was growing as the hours passed and those who could leave the clinic drove around the base searching for her. However, no one saw Jackie or her yellow bike.

The following morning, when there was still no word or communication from Jackie, Lt Commander Willie Ewing, one of the Staff Medical Doctors at the Naval Air Station, organized a search team of about ten available military personnel from the hospital to try and find her. By then they all knew something was drastically wrong, and decided to take it upon themselves to find out why she failed to show up for work or never went home. They concentrated their efforts along the banks of the Kings River as someone mentioned Jackie had previously ridden her bike out there. It was a beautiful area with the river and trees and a nice cool place to relax and study. The Navy people at the base called it the "Marina" although there was not much there, just a place for people to hang out and cool off from the heat, but military people have a way of making the best of what they have when they are far away from home.

In the early afternoon of October 6, 1980, at 12:10 PM, the body of twenty-four year old HM2 Jacqueline Jane Wurst, U.S. Navy, was found by the Navy search party floating in the water near the area of a peaceful looking shady cove of the river. She had been hit on the head twice, and marks on her neck indicated she had been strangled, possibly with a rope, then thrown into the river, just below a knoll with a very large Cottonwood tree beside the bank. Her shorts had been removed and her blouse and undergarments cut away, and there was a piece of rope across her right wrist. Later, Kings County Coroner David Moore reported she died from asphyxiation due to strangulation and she had been sexually assaulted. She also had multiple injuries indicating she had fought viciously for her life to the very end. Her yellow ten-speed bike was still parked where she had left it on top the knoll. Her backpack, books, and watch were found strewn about the area.

After Jackie was found Navy Officials at the base were notified and they then called the Kings County Sheriff's Office. Sheriff's investigators were brought in to conduct the investigation since the crime had been committed off the military base and Detective Larry Orth and Deputy Darryl Henry were assigned the investigation. Information later pieced together indicated she had left the base at approximately 2 PM on her yellow bike heading for the Kings River. Jackie normally didn't ride her bike to work, but that day her car had broken down and she had ridden her bike from her apartment in town to the base, which was about a sixteen mile round trip. She was exceptionally physically fit stemming from a lifetime of work on a farm as well as enjoying anything sports oriented, so the bike ride was an easy thing for her.

The Hanford Sentinel, one of the newspapers for the local area, reported Jackie was from Osceola, Wisconsin, had joined the U.S.

Navy in August 1976 and had been assigned to the Lemoore Naval Air Station since August 1979. She was identified as a Second Class Petty Officer, HM2, and in addition to her duties at the hospital emergency room was active in the station softball program. She had recently been selected as Overall Female Athlete at the base for the fourth quarter. She was survived by her parents, two brothers and two sisters living in the Wisconsin area.

The *Sentinel* also reported that on the following Thursday, a memorial service was held to honor Jackie and to help those who knew her draw strength from each other, and to possibly find an answer to the question they all wanted answered. Why did this happen? It was reported that about two hundred-fifty persons attended the service in the Base Chapel and heard her described as a quiet but friendly person who was dedicated to her hospital duties. The day of the service the Command ordered the flag flown at half-staff to honor her.

As the base chaplain and local ministers sought to comfort those present, some cried while others tried hard not to, but they all listened as they remembered better times. All recalled her as dedicated to both her job and her faith. The common spoken word described Jackie as always pleasant, with a wonderful smile and one who maintained dignity throughout her short life.

The Commander of the Base Hospital said "Jackie was the epitome of an ideal corpsman" and was held in "high esteem" by both co-workers and her patients. He shared the outrage that such a beautiful young woman met such a violent death on a peaceful Sunday in the Navy community. He noted she had planned to pursue a nursing degree after her discharge the following summer. He said her murder "reflects the all too often violent behavior of the society in which we live."

The minister from the local Lutheran Church which Jackie attended remarked, "Lives that are touched by tragedy can find the strength to go on … I don't know why this has happened, but God knows and loves and forgives and gives…"

The local Navy Chaplain summed it up best when he told those in attendance not to consider the length of Jackie's life, but rather the quality. "Some of the most beautiful things on earth don't last long," he said pointing to flowers and sunrises. He added, "God places more importance on the quality than the quantity of life. The best evidence of quality in life is seen when a person is willing to use their life for a good purpose." The Chaplain then asked all to remember, "Jacqueline is really with the Lord and to honor her not because she died, but because of the way she lived."

Those words rang true again when almost twenty-five years later I contacted Jackie's mother, Phyllis Wurst, and told her I wanted to write a story of Jackie's life as a tribute to her. Her answer together with Jackie's father was a simple "yes"---they wanted their daughter's story told. Again, they pointed out although Jackie's life was short what mattered most was God places more importance on the quality rather than the quantity of life. Those family convictions compelled me to move forward with the story.

CHAPTER 2

IMPACT OF MURDER FELT—

Media inquiries at first revealed military personnel were concerned the murder might reflect adversely on the air station. Each person emphasized it did not happen on the base, but took place during the daytime at a recreational family spot popular with the local populace as well as the Navy family. Hospital staff that knew Jackie were all visibly shaken when questioned about the murder. They all expressed fear, frustration and anger stating they did not understand why this had happened and who would have wanted to hurt Jackie. The impact from her death caused her former co-workers to be more cautious and wary while being more protective of their friends. Many in the Navy community were young and had never before experienced a violent death of someone like themselves, and especially one so well liked by all that knew her.

Various newspaper articles written in the local *Hanford Sentinel* told of how her close friends were dealing with this terrible tragedy. One friend told of how Jackie was planning to go back to school and how she wanted to challenge the LVN (licensed vocational nurse) test before she got out of the Navy. Some states will allow one to take the test for LVN and if one can pass they will receive the LVN certification based on their test results and previous experience. Jackie had not only gone to Corps School but she had also worked in the various hospital wards and in intensive care. She had also taken many extra courses required by the military to maintain the standards of training.

Jackie's friend also described her as someone easy to talk to and if you had a problem she made you feel at ease, like a lifelong friend. She would listen and then give advice. She loved to cook and a big thing for her was banana bread. The friend said in 1979, either at Thanksgiving or Christmas—she couldn't remember which—they both had the duty and had to work the holiday, so they made four loaves of banana bread and took them to the hospital for the duty crew that day.

While Jackie loved being with people and enjoyed athletics she also liked her privacy. She had shared an apartment off base with a roommate until about six weeks before her murder. When the roommate moved on she discussed with a friend whether or not to get a new roommate, and then decided against it as she enjoyed living alone and being able to read and listen to music whenever she wanted, both which she loved to do. This same friend when questioned told investigators she didn't believe it was anyone who knew Jackie that had murdered her. She just couldn't see how anyone who knew her would want to harm her as she was warm and well liked by everyone. She said it made her mad when she thought about the person who would have done it and as far as suspicions, she didn't have any and she tried hard not to think about the murder as it made her angry.

One newspaper article in the *Hanford Sentinel* told of a friend, "Tom", who had been stationed in Japan with Jackie before they had both been transferred to Lemoore. He had been a good friend of Jackie's boyfriend in Japan. He said after the murder happened it drew everyone at the hospital closer together. He told how one day soon after the murder he had gone to pick up his girlfriend at school and she had already left. He said he found himself panicky until he found out where she was and that she was okay. He said he just overreacted because of what had happened.

"Tom" also said he used to go on bicycle rides with Jackie and the weekend before her death he had taken her out to the Marina. It was such a beautiful place in the spring and in the fall, and she didn't even know about the area until he took her there. He said they talked about their time together in Japan and about getting out of the Navy and the high crime rate. How in Atlanta, Georgia, there had been more than fifteen black children recently killed. He said they talked about the crime rate in Japan and how there it was almost non-existent. People didn't even have to worry about locking their cars or their homes.

He said he didn't believe in capital punishment but he thought our judicial system needed to be changed. In Japan punishment for crime is very severe and here it is almost like nothing, he believed. He also said the attitude of the majority of the people on the base had changed and now they were much more protective. "Tom" also said he didn't know whether it was because of the military or what, but in the hospital people tended to be more like family. You work so closely together.

Another newspaper article also told of an interview with "Ann". She told how the girls who had cars on base would drive to work even though it was easy walking distance. She also talked about self-defense classes and how "I don't carry anything with me. I hate to think about having to. I was thinking about all this stuff …isn't there anything I can do, like could they use me as a decoy or anything to catch the suspect?"

Other people told of not going anywhere alone, on-base or off-base. Some said they would never go out to the Marina again. One very close young friend said she had "taken care of business she had never thought about before. I had my will drawn up and made available to my parents." The fear was in all of them and they were constantly looking over their shoulders. This horrible crime wasn't supposed to happen in an area of good, wholesome young people. The uneasiness affected everyone at Lemoore Naval Air Station, civilians and military. This was too close to home.

Chapter 3
The case goes cold—

Kings County Sheriff's Deputies questioned co-workers and associates of Jackie's into the early morning hours seeking any information which could lead them to a possible suspect. Everyone they talked to was at a loss as to who could have committed such a terrible crime. The Kings County's Secret Witness program posted a reward for information leading to the arrest and conviction of her killer hoping to receive tips to aid in the investigation. The County Sheriff put a clamp on the release of information concerning the crime because of what he claimed may have been damaging news leaks to the media.

Since the crime occurred off base and in a civilian area the local Sheriff's Department assumed control of the case. Detective Orth who was handling the case was a well seasoned, no nonsense, dedicated investigator who was highly respected for his integrity. However, since the Sheriff had no jurisdiction on the military base, investigators from the Naval Investigative Service (NIS) were also working the case jointly from the military end. NIS is a world wide organization with field satellite offices throughout the world and with Special Agents highly trained as investigators, forensic experts, security specialists and analysts, assigned to those various locations. Special Agents were interviewing all her friends and co-workers to determine if anyone could have had a grudge against her or knew anyone who possibly could be involved. NIS also was sending leads out to the other bases where she had previously been assigned in hopes of getting some bit of information that would help. Due to the transient nature of the Navy personnel, leads were sent to bases and ships throughout the world, to wherever they were transferred. However, those interviews and inquiries failed to provide any viable information which would identify a suspect.

Detective Larry Orth, Kings County Sheriff's Department 1980

When the lead reached the NIS office in Japan, information was relayed back to Lemoore that on June 24, 1978, when Jackie had been stationed in Yokosuka, Japan, she had been the victim of a sexual assault. She had been asleep in the Bachelor Enlisted Quarters (BEQ) that night when someone entered her room and assaulted her. Because of the severity of the case a task force consisting of Special Agents Robert Kohlmeyer, Wendell Taguchi, C. D. Mugglesworth, Jim Vorse and Steve Spears had been formed to investigate this assault, along with a number of other similar cases which had happened in other locations in Japan. The junior investigator was Taguchi and he was fortunate to be able to lift a latent fingerprint from the door knob, and from that they were able to identify a transient sailor from a ship in port at the time. The sailor was later tried by General Court-martial, convicted, sentenced to a long prison term and given a dishonorable discharge. With this information investigators started making inquiries to see if this person had somehow been released early from prison and could possibly have committed the murder. However, it was found that he was still in prison and therefore not a suspect in the murder case.

Even Jackie's co-workers and close friends in Japan were questioned regarding her murder. Her boyfriend in Japan was also questioned which was quite difficult for him, as he kept saying how could he have done it as he was in Japan at the time? Letters that she had written to him were taken into evidence even though he felt they had no relevance to the incident.

A senior ranking medical officer when interviewed by NIS remarked how he thought one of the Navy personnel who first spotted Jackie's body in the water acted strange. When he spotted the body, instead of going directly to it to see if she were alive, he just sat down on the grass and was crying and yelling for someone else to come to the scene. The officer felt since he was also a senior medical person he should have reacted differently. This all bothered the officer and made him wonder about this person; since he found her, and reacted so strangely, could he have been involved?

I had been made aware of the murder when it first happened, as I was a Special Agent with NIS assigned to the headquarters staff for the 12th Naval District located at Treasure Island, near San Francisco, California. Whenever a major case broke within our own district staff personnel were all informed. Amongst my duties which included criminal investigations, I had a specialty of being the Regional Polygraph

Examiner, with my jurisdiction covering the area from Northern California to the Aleutian chain to Hawaii, and sometimes points beyond that. When I first read the report I was stunned because I remembered the name "Jackie Wurst" from the incident that had happened earlier in Japan. When that assault happened I was just finishing a five year tour in Japan and was in the process of rotating back to Treasure Island. The case stuck in my mind because of it involving a young Navy hospital corpsman originally from Wisconsin, which was also my home state, and our office handling the case and quickly finding the perpetrator. I remembered I had congratulated the case investigators on a quick resolution, and a week later I rotated from Japan to the United States.

Since my primary duty was to interview and polygraph subjects, it was requested that I conduct a polygraph examination on the person who was first on the murder scene to determine if he was involved in any way, because of what was felt to be unusual behavior at the time. I brought the person of interest into the NIS office and began to interview him. The young man just sat there and kept saying, "It was my fault, it was my fault." When asked if he was involved he wouldn't say yes nor deny it. Finally he was asked to submit to a polygraph which he did voluntarily. The polygraph results showed there was no deception and that he was neither involved nor committed the crime. During the post test interview he finally was able to explain he was the one who had taken her out to the Marina the week before and shown her the area. He just felt totally responsible for having taken her there, and believed if he had not done so she would still be alive. He had also known her when they had been stationed together in Japan and had a lot of fond memories during that timeframe. He was very fond of her as a good friend, and the horror of finding her as he did was almost more than he could handle.

Aerial view of crime scene. Photograph taken October 6, 1980 in Lemoore, California

As the Regional Polygraph Agent I was traveling constantly from one military base to another conducting my assignments. I always felt the person who committed the murder was a transient Navy person that moved from air station to air station with the squadrons, and who immediately after committing the murder had moved on to another location. Those squadrons were stationed at five different locations: Adak, Alaska; Whidbey Island, Washington; Alameda, Moffet Field and Lemoore, California. Whenever I was at any one of those locations I constantly had this case in the back of my mind, hoping to pick up some bit of information which would give us the lead we needed to find the killer. I looked for similar crimes committed with similar circumstances. I thought over and over, "It has to be a transient; it has to be someone who was there one day – the day of the murder – and then gone the next, shipped out to his next duty station with a mobile unit." There were even times when people said to me to forget the murder as there was plenty of other work to be done. That was all very true as we were handling all crimes committed by Navy and Marine Corps personnel, plus mountains of other work for which we were responsible. But in the back of my mind was constantly the thought that someday I just might run across someone who had some bit of information regarding Jackie's murder. I just thought how could such a wholesome young lady whom everyone loved and who had a wonderful future ahead of her, be victimized twice and then her killer get away with it. We had to find the killer!

As 1980 was drawing to a close, the *Hanford Sentinel* was still publishing articles regarding the case to keep the public informed as to the status of the investigation. But there was nothing new to report. Every homicide investigator will tell you it is imperative to identify and locate a suspect in a homicide as quickly as possible after a crime has been committed. The longer it takes the more difficult it becomes as memories become foggy or even forgotten or people move away. In this case, multitudes of people had been located and interviewed, but no viable or productive leads had developed and no logical suspects identified. People were beginning to fear the case would never be solved. The case just seemed to have gone dry as soon as it began.

In October of 1981, Jackie's parents wrote to the Sheriff's office requesting personal items of Jackie's that had been seized as evidence, and also for any information regarding the status of the case. On October 22, Detective Larry Orth responded back informing the family each piece of evidence was very important, and he was still unable to release the items. He went on to explain how every piece would be important when the person responsible was found, and how they did not want to lose the case later on in the courts because of missing evidence.

He then went on and expressed his condolences and explained how difficult it was to write to the parents of a homicide victim. He explained he wished he could tell them they had apprehended the persons responsible for Jackie's death, but he couldn't. He also said, "I can guarantee you one thing, we will never give up looking for Jackie's killer or killers."

Forensic evidence had been analyzed and results returned from the laboratories but unfortunately DNA was not yet available in those years as an investigative tool. Even with the Kings County Secret Witness program no one came forward with pertinent information on the case. The investigation reached into the New Year and entered the dormant investigative stage, making it more difficult. As more time passed the frustration for all involved grew, knowing it was possible this investigation might become a "cold case" which would languish in the files, unresolved for years to come, in spite of the efforts of all who worked so diligently. The dogged efforts of the NIS personnel, Detective Larry Orth's persistence in seeking information, my own pursuit of just some small shred of knowledge from anyone which would lead us to the truth----all these efforts still failed to turn up a suspect and the case was cold.

Chapter 4
What was this place called "Lemoore"?

What was this place called "Lemoore"? Why was this Naval Air Station in such a "desolate" area? The first most people ever heard of this area was in John Steinbeck's novel, *The Grapes of Wrath*. In his book he told of the lives of a family who were victims of social and economic depression, who traveled from Oklahoma along Route 66, then up California State Highway 99, into the San Joaquin Valley. The valley north of Bakersfield was a lush agricultural land, and gave hope to those seeking the "Promised Land of California" during those harsh years. Almost thirty years later another generation, this time officers, naval aviators, sailors, men, women and children, would be facing similar experiences of worry and a vision of hope at the Lemoore Naval Air Station, as they lived through the Vietnam Conflict.

This almost dead-center location in California was a prime location for a large master jet base from the perspective of Navy officials. The Chief of Naval Operations reviewed five sites in California and Nevada for potential development and with the strong cooperation of local city officials Lemoore was the logical choice. The increasing population growth in the San Diego and San Francisco areas, and the inevitable encroachment on other Navy/Marine Corps air stations on the west coast required the Navy to build a new facility with the ability to support 50 percent of all fleet aviation units in the Pacific area.

In August 1956, President Eisenhower signed documents for $81 million dollars to purchase 31,000 acres of land for a modern jet base and construction began in 1958 on two 13,500 feet long parallel runways. Base housing for eight hundred single-family units was projected to be built, and eventually a six mile long freeway between the city of Lemoore and the main gate of the air station was constructed. On July 8, 1961, the commissioning ceremonies of Lemoore Naval Air Station were held and that day the main gate opened to forty thousand visiting vehicles.

The fleet squadrons, with pilots, supporting maintenance personnel and their families arrived at Lemoore and because of the number of personnel needed to operate the air station many of the men, women and their families lived off base in the local areas. The remoteness of the San Joaquin Valley and the long dismal periods of thick fog during the winter months were very difficult for many to cope. The closest medium-size city was Fresno, about thirty miles north, and during those foggy winter months driving there was almost impossible. The isolation, the weather (which besides being cold and foggy in the winter was very hot in the summer) and the stress of the work were causes to build strong support groups between the military members, their families, and the community outside the base gates.

During the Vietnam Conflict the wartime schedule for the pilots, sailors, and families was extremely demanding and during a single period they had twelve squadrons deployed at-sea. One hundred-thirty pilots from the air station were shot-down in combat; eighty-seven of those were classified as prisoners-of-war or missing-in-action with only forty-three being returned from captivity. Lieutenant Junior-

Grade Everett Alvarez was assigned to the squadron VA-144 and was the first Navy pilot captured in Vietnam, and was held prisoner in North Vietnam for 8 1/2 years. The first Navy pilot killed-in-action in Vietnam was Lieutenant Junior-Grade Dick Sather and he also was from a squadron at Lemoore. Commander James Stockdale, Commander of the Air Group-16, (CAG-16) from Lemoore, was shot-down over North Vietnam and was a POW for eight years. He earned two Purple Hearts, four Silver Stars, and the Medal of Honor and was later promoted to Vice Admiral.

During this time there was the constant fear in the military families of an official black Navy sedan stopping in front of their home, bringing the tragic news of combat loss. One of my long time navy friends, Mike Boston, Captain, USN, (Retired), was an aviator assigned to one of the squadrons at Lemoore during 1969-71 and his wife Sandi still remembers those days. One vivid memory she has is of one afternoon when she was out in her front yard with her three children. Her two daughters went next door to play and Sandi was sitting and relaxing with her baby when a black car pulled into their cul-de-sac. Sandi immediately rushed into the house and closed the door. She sank into a rocking chair and started rocking the baby back and forth and ignored the banging on the front door; her rationale being if she didn't answer the door she wouldn't get bad news. When she no longer could take the noise she opened the door to find it was only her girls coming home for dinner. To this day she can't tell how long she was rocking in the chair and the memories still bring tears.

Sandi also remembers another wife's husband had been listed as missing-in-action (MIA) for quite some time. One day she heard the mail slot on the front door slam. She went and picked up the mail and in it was a letter with Vietnamese post marks and postage. She fell to the floor speechless, not knowing just what to do. When she opened the letter, it was from her husband who, as it turned out, was a prisoner-of-war (POW). This was the first she had heard of his capture and the Navy also was unaware until she received the letter and notified them. Her husband was later repatriated and went on to command a squadron and a naval air station until his retirement. Some of the wives never got such news.

One day Sandi had gone shopping at a store in Lemoore and when she got to the check-out stand she realized she had forgotten her checkbook. She asked the clerk if she could leave the items at the store and come right back and pay. The total was about $50 which was a lot in those days. The clerk said, "...take the goods, you're from the base, you can pay me next time you're in town." The positive relationship between the base and the community was remarkable. This was the base where Jackie Wurst was assigned to the Naval Hospital in August 1979, when she left Japan.

Chapter 5

Tom Brannon-Special Agent, U.S. Naval Investigative Service

Like Jackie, I too had come from Wisconsin. My Irish parents part of the endless migration from the mid-west to California after World War II. Irish families have always been matriarchal, and my grandmother McClung was ours. A strong, tiny Irish lady who could cook a five course meal at age ninety, she ruled the roost. In 1952 she moved from Kenosha, Wisconsin, where we were all living, to Los Angeles to help my aunt with her new baby. Our family soon followed, and I was almost sixteen years old and thoroughly miserable. From a town where I knew everyone and had the eye of every girl in Kenosha, I became just another outsider at Glendale High School.

After biking the streets of our factory town, stopping in every shop to say hello and knowing every nun in our parish, I had now become dependent on my mom for transportation. I was desperate for a car like the rest of the California high school boys, and a return to my freedom which I knew could only be obtained by money. My dad had taught me to work hard at any job I could find – so it was midnight bakery boy, soda jerk, and gas station flunky. I did anything I could find to make money to buy myself a car and pay for the gas. Our family settled into a small neat house in the city of Glendale. We had a patch of grass out front, a driveway and two palm trees in the parkway---that California dream! Still, as soon as I finished high school I joined the Navy as I knew I was required to fill my military obligation, and also, the Navy would give me the chance to travel.

Author and wife (Editor) in 1980

As a raw eighteen-year old on the USS Worcester (CL-144), I didn't find investigative work right away. Instead, I discovered how much I liked seeing the world. Like many a new Californian before me and after me, something about being uprooted as a youngster stuck in my nature, and as my ship docked at ports across Southeast Asia I grew to love it. By the time I left the service in 1957, I knew I wanted more of that adventure. Working odd jobs back in Glendale, I heard about an opening in the Police Department and got myself downtown to take their entrance exam and was hired.

In those days, a new policeman could drive a cruiser and stop crime with just a high school diploma and plain old grit. I had my share of it all, driving the highly lit streets of our city and answering calls for things like "211 Robbery in Progress". Most of the time these were false alarms, but occasionally, we actually had to chase someone, trying hard to shoot straight and still missing, as young and scared as the fool thieves we were after. After three years of this, going to college at nights, and working at the gas station in my off hours, my ears were still tuned for new opportunities. I heard the old cops talking about the Office of Naval Intelligence in Los Angeles hiring civilian Special Agents. Once again I got myself downtown and applied, but found I would have to wait another year before the lengthy application process would be complete. By the spring of 1962 though, I was in.

The Office of Naval Intelligence (ONI) was first established in 1882, by then Secretary of Navy William Hunt, with various tasks including collecting information regarding foreign vessels, and overseas plants and shipyards. In later years, ONI's responsibilities were expanded to include espionage, sabotage and all investigations of the Navy's potential adversaries. In 1966 the name Naval Investigative Service (NIS) was adapted and NIS was working more criminal investigations and counterintelligence. In 1992 the name was again changed to Naval Criminal Investigative Service, (NCIS). With each of these name changes the mission of the agency was expanded and restructured and the Special Agents working for the agency continued to give their full support to the Navy and Marine Corps.

In the early years of the organization the agents came from all backgrounds. Some were former police officers like me, some former military aviators or ship drivers, and some were intellectuals from the best schools in the country. Many an Ivy Leaguer came to the government agencies in those days because it offered travel, intrigue and camaraderie. I had finally found that worldly frontier I liked so much as a sailor, but now without the low rank and sea duties, I began to take full advantage. After training at the Office of Naval Intelligence Academy in Washington D.C., I became a full-fledged Special Agent. I began to have some responsibility for investigations and learned another fact about myself—I could talk the truth out of about anyone. More and more I talked young sailors into confessing their petty crimes, from stealing the mess fund to knifing a buddy. I was twenty-eight years old, a civilian with the U.S. Navy and the Vietnam War was just heating up.

My dad had been a metallurgist for the War Department during World War II, and we had a good old fashioned family commitment to serving our country. My older brother had joined the Marines to get out of Glendale and was now serving in Vietnam, earning a decoration already. My younger brother had also done a tour in Vietnam. I put two and two together and saw where I could follow my family's example, get ahead fast, and earn extra pay.

I volunteered for service in Vietnam as a civilian Special Agent and arrived in Saigon on March 7th, 1965, where I was to be an investigator of crimes amongst Navy and Marine Corps personnel. However, within my first week I was walking through the wreckage of the bombed U.S. Embassy in Saigon, looking for signs of Vietcong. My talent at getting the truth out of people was now more than a good job; it was Intelligence. For the next thirteen years I crisscrossed the oceans and islands of the Far East, investigating simple crimes and capital ones, internal and treasonous, as I developed my ability to uncover the true motivations of Navy/Marine personnel as they wandered astray. I was now forty-one years old, and once again Uncle Sam sent orders for me and my family to move, this time back to the United States.

In 1978 when I left Yokosuka, Japan, I had been with Naval Investigative Service sixteen years, and I was given a plum assignment back to the 12th Naval District Headquarters at Treasure Island, in the San Francisco Bay. My wife and I bought a beautiful house in the east bay. We repainted, landscaped, and refinished and turned it into a showplace. To us it was important to have everything done as quickly as possible in order to be able to enjoy it, since in my line of work one never knew how long one would be assigned to the same location. Now, still as a Special Agent, but also with the specialty as the Regional Polygraph Examiner on the northwest coast, I was extremely busy traveling my territory, conducting interviews of suspects and witnesses, doing interrogations, and administering polygraph examinations.

Lemoore Naval Air Station was part of the area I covered. It was – and is - in the San Joaquin Valley of Central California, the great inner valley that runs from north of the hills that surround Los Angeles, all the way up to where it meets the Sacramento valley. This area is in the heart of California and is the state's top agricultural producing region. Sometimes referred to as "the nation's salad bowl". Lemoore, just west of Visalia, is in the middle of this flat, dry, fertile basin, and still in 1980, this was the middle of no where. *Tuleville*, we called it when I was young; a California term which probably originated from the Tule plants indigenous to the area, but to us it meant in the middle of no where. That year I would learn Lemoore was where Jackie Wurst had been sent for her second assignment as a hospital corpsman, when I received a call to come help with an investigation into her murder.

CHAPTER 6
THAT ACRONYM SET THE STAGE—

On late Sunday afternoon of May 11, 1982, while sitting in our kitchen in Lafayette, California, having a cup of coffee and reading the newspaper, I read an article regarding a rape which had just occurred in a neighboring city. A young college coed had been grabbed from behind a clump of bushes and sexually assaulted. During the course of the rape she had bit down on the suspect's tongue and kneed him in the groin, at the same time causing him to jerk back which resulted in a rip to his tongue. The victim spit out the tongue and the suspect fled from the scene bleeding profusely. She also had been confined with a rope attached to her wrist.

NIS Special Agent Greg Redfern to this day remembers receiving a call to respond with local police to a claim that a sailor had been assaulted in the Oakland-Alameda tube. "Tube" is the local terminology used for a tunnel which goes between the two cities. The sailor claimed he was driving his rental car when he was jumped at the entrance of the tube, on the Oakland side, and assaulted. He said when the guy hit him in the jaw it caused him to bite down hard on his tongue and cause the injury. While he was being treated at the Oak Knoll Naval Hospital an All Points Bulletin (APB) was issued to be on the lookout for a rape suspect with a tongue injury. At that point the local police arrested the suspect and then turned him over to Navy Military Police. He was then returned to Legal Hold status pending adjudication for additional rapes in the Bay Area he had allegedly committed. Greg Redfern still remembers the case due to the unusual nature of the incident, and says the petite Hispanic female who was the true victim, was truly heroic in her actions and also was a "dynamite" witness.

The nature of this incident made headlines in the local media and they reported that a sailor identified as an "aviation rate (AD2)" had allegedly committed the rape. To anyone else, except someone who had both been in the Navy and also had worked for them, that acronym, "AD2", would have no meaning at all. To me, it was the most important thing I had read in the newspaper ---and also there was the rope around the wrist. There had to be some connection----the MO was similar--- could it possibly be?

Seventeen months after Jackie's murder, some two hundred miles from the crime scene, and again on a quiet Sunday afternoon, I thought this might be the break in the case we desperately needed. On Monday morning after arriving at work, the first thing I did was make a telephone call to the Naval Air Station Alameda, which was the location where the perpetrator was being held by the Navy. When I learned of those additional rapes he had been charged with, I knew this person was definitely worth checking out. I talked with a Navy yeoman and asked her to check the sailor's military record (SRB) and tell me where he had been assigned on October 5, 1980. When she came back to me and said, "Mr. Brannon, he was in Lemoore, California on that date," I believed he could have been involved---but proving it would be another matter.

Kenneth Bailey had been out on bail for multiple rapes and had legal counsel representing him which would prevent him from being interrogated without counsel being present. Investigations are never easy but this one would prove to be extremely difficult for many reasons. Many factors entered into the investigation, one of which being the murder victim had been thrown into the water and it was likely there was contamination of forensic evidence as a result. In later years it was said if DNA had been available at the time, this investigation would have been a closed matter from the beginning because of other forensic evidence found. Detective Larry Orth many years later did tell me he believed the Attorney for Bailey was aware DNA was coming into prominence and with the other evidence such as blood and semen found at the scene, it was logical to assume Bailey would have been identified.

Without being able to talk to the suspect Bailey, and without the benefit of the forensic evidence, our task was just beginning to prove whether or not Bailey was our prime suspect. NIS investigators began their work by sending out leads to the various locations where Bailey had been assigned since the murder, in order to locate people who knew him. Perhaps someone would have some bit of information---perhaps some comment Bailey would have made which would indicate an involvement.

We interviewed anyone we could find who had known Bailey—coworkers, best friends, girl friends. They all said they had no knowledge of his involvement in the murder; he had never mentioned any connection to it. One particular sailor located in Orlando, Florida, however did provide an interesting fact. He stated during 1980 he had been assigned to the squadron, VA-146, at Lemoore, and had been aboard the USS Constellation while it was deployed to the Philippines in September 1980. He went on to say he was not part of the advance party which returned home, however fifteen to twenty individuals, including Bailey, flew back to San Francisco early on approximately

Sept 22, at which time they rented cars and drove back to Lemoore. This individual also stated he knew Bailey subsequently took leave and drove his personal car back to the Bay Area where he had relatives residing. The interviewee then said he, himself, had not arrived back in the United States until October 22-23. He then stated he became aware of the rape/murder of the victim through a newspaper article but he had never spoken to Bailey regarding the incident. He said he didn't remember any bandages on Bailey but Bailey had been involved in several fights with other personnel in his department during the period he knew him.

One of Bailey's close friends, "Steven Smith", (not his real name in order to protect his identity) a Yeoman 2nd Class (YN2), was interviewed in Korea where he was currently stationed. He said he did not have any information regarding Bailey being involved in the murder nor did he think it possible he could have done such a thing. He did say Bailey had been to his house for dinner on October 5, 1980, but he didn't notice anything unusual or out of order with Bailey---no visible scratches or bruises. There were also a few inconsistencies in his statement but the important item was the fact he had seen Bailey on the day of the murder. He ended his interview by saying he had no knowledge of Bailey being involved in the murder nor was he, himself, involved.

Because of the inconsistencies and the fact Bailey had been to his house on the day of the murder, NIS Agents felt if they could bring "Smith" back from Korea and talk to him here in the local office, perhaps he would provide more information. The NIS office in Lemoore briefed the Navy Judge Advocate General (JAG) and requested the return of "Smith" to the United States for further interview. Rear Admiral James Busey at that time was Commander, Pacific Fleet Light Attack Wing, and he gave permission for the further interview process to be conducted. This authorization from Admiral Busey provided NIS the opportunity to obtain a statement from a material witness which later confirmed the identity of the perpetrator who killed Jackie Wurst. My thanks will always go out to Admiral Busey for making the decision to return "Smith" to the base at Lemoore.

On February 23, 1983, NIS Special Agent H. H. Kimball, a well respected agent and former California Highway Patrolman, and Detective Larry Orth, interviewed "Smith" in Lemoore. "Smith" again related how the squadron personnel had all rotated back from the Southeast Asia cruise. How Bailey came by his house and they all made plans for Bailey and his girlfriend "Sue" to come for dinner on October 5th. He told how they tried to arrange the dinner for the prior weekend but couldn't manage to get their schedules together so made it for the second weekend they were back from the cruise. "Smith" said Bailey and "Sue" probably arrived around 6:30 PM and would have eaten around seven or eight, which was normally the time his wife served dinner when they had guests. He said he didn't recall any unusual attitude changes when Bailey was there---nothing out of the ordinary that he could remember.

He said he and Bailey were quite close friends and Bailey associated also with his family. He told how Bailey and his wife were separated and planning on getting a divorce and Bailey was discreetly seeing "Sue" who was still married to another sailor. "Smith" told of how he was so surprised when he was in Korea and heard Bailey had been convicted of rape since he didn't think he was capable of such a crime. He did say Bailey's mood's changed frequently and he was what he considered "impulsive" and he did think that he "hit his wife" because he once said he got so mad at her he could hit her. "Smith" also said one time the wife came into the office of the Commanding Officer and talked with the CO, but he didn't know what they talked about.

He didn't know about his carrying a knife of any kind but was aware he had purchased a .32 caliber automatic pistol, which he carried in his car, as he had seen it several times before they all went out on the cruise. "Smith" again stated he didn't recall seeing any scratches on Bailey's face. He then went on to say how he thought it was his own wife who had mentioned the murder at the dinner party, and some comment about how insecure the base was, and how someone could just come over the fence and break into a house. He then stated he could provide no additional relevant information regarding the investigation.

When the NIS office and the Sheriff's office had concluded their interview of "Smith" they called me and said they believed he had no further relevant information to disclose. At that point it was requested by the NIS office that I conduct a polygraph examination to ascertain he was telling the truth. I was some two hundred miles away and extremely busy with other work that week, therefore arrangements were made with Navy personnel to bring "Smith" to the Andersen's Pea Soup Restaurant on Highway 5 in Santa Nella, that being a half-way location between my office and theirs. I reserved a room in the adjoining hotel to be used as my temporary office, and started down the highway. All the way there, I kept trying to think how I could approach "Smith" in a way which would convince him to give up any information he was possibly withholding on his best friend.

On February 24, 1983, I met with "Smith" and advised him he was suspected of withholding information concerning the homicide of Jackie Wurst and/or participation in the homicide. "Smith" signed a waiver stating he understood his rights and did not desire to have a lawyer present at the time. I began the interview by telling "Smith" of the actual murder and how viciously the girl had been attacked. I told him regardless of Bailey being his best friend he had to consider what Bailey had done---that Bailey was not only a convicted rapist but now he was also a killer. After about three hours of talking, talking and talking, "Smith" finally agreed to tell what he knew. He then signed a voluntary sworn statement detailing what Bailey had actually told him on October 5th, 1980.

CHAPTER 7
I KNEW HE WAS TELLING
THE TRUTH—

The following information is taken directly from "Smith's" statement. Although, not the complete statement, it is not taken out of context nor is it written in any manner as to misconstrue what was said. Certain comments are merely deleted because of being repetitious or later proven to be fabrications and contradicted by evidence, in order to be sensitive to the memory of Jackie Wurst and to her family.

"Bailey is like a brother to myself and is probably my closest friend. I have kept this information that I am about to relate bottled up in my mind for over two years but now I want to tell the truth as I know it from what I was told by Bailey.

"Bailey came to my house in Lemoore about 18:30 on 5 October 1980. I recall that date because Kenny Bailey was supposed to come to my house the previous weekend and could not. So he came on the evening of 5 Oct 1980. Also, I heard all over the base the next day of the death of a former HM2 Jackie Wurst, USN, who was found murdered at Lemoore, CA. When Bailey arrived at my house I immediately noticed a gauze pad on his right side of the face. I asked Bailey what happened and he said that he had been in a fight.

"We went outside to talk about it and I saw that Bailey was upset over something. Bailey stated over and over again, 'I can't believe I did it.' He repeated himself to me again and again. I asked him what he was talking about. Bailey stated to me while we were alone in my back yard 'I killed her', referring to Jackie. I was shocked. .... Bailey then described that he killed Wurst at Kings River, which is located outside the back gate at NAS Lemoore. Bailey at this time had tears in his eyes and stated 'I did not mean to do it', meaning kill Jackie. Bailey said this over and over again to me at the time. ...Bailey was so upset that I went inside of my house and got two beers to calm him and me down at this time. ...Bailey also stated to me while talking about his having killed Jackie that he was going to his car and get his gun which he kept in his car, a 1978 Mustang. It was a .32 cal. automatic weapon, make unknown. Bailey stated that he was going to take his gun to his head and blow his brains out. It was obvious to me that Bailey was distraught over what he had done....

"During this conversation Bailey stated 'I know that she is dead.' I asked him why, meaning what or how did it happen. Then I stated to Bailey I knew your temper would get you in trouble, you f...... hot head. I took Bailey's gun that night and drove him home. I learned the next day that Wurst's body was found where he said he had killed her. That date was 6 Oct 1980. Bailey seemed to disappear for awhile after this timeframe and I could not locate him.

"I again saw Bailey on 16 Oct 80, the date I recall because it was the day after payday. Bailey came to personnel inquiring about his pay. I again at this time discussed with Bailey the circumstances of Wurst's death. This time I tried to convince Bailey to turn himself in but he gave that Bailey look which I took to mean no f...... way. I feel he felt that he had not been caught for killing Jackie and he might get away with it.

"Bailey at this time described his encounter with Wurst. He had known Jackie before and lived near her and indicated he met her before at a supermarket in Lemoore......Anyway Bailey's account of the incident was ...when he said he got to Kings River he tried to put the make on Wurst. This took place according to Bailey in his 1978 Mustang, yellow in color. Bailey said he got out of the car and tackled her at the Kings River. According to Bailey, Wurst started screaming and resisted, was fighting and kicking and it was described to me like a 'slug fest'. Bailey then said he put his hands around her throat to shut her up. Bailey then told me that he blacked out after this, but he knew she was dead.

"I did not discuss the incident with Bailey after this as Bailey said he did not want to discuss it further. I did read after this that Wurst had been murdered and there was a reward. I read an account of the incident in the *Golden Eagle* and the *Hanford Sentinel*. I also knew and saw Bailey carry a straight razor and had seen it in his possession a long time previous to this incident. I also know that twine was present in the work spaces where Bailey worked at the power plants. I can describe the rope as a shiny nylon type twine. The rope was used by the AD rates or anyone who worked on the aircraft at the hangar.

"I was interviewed previously by NIS in Korea on two occasions and once by the Kings County Sheriff's department. I did not tell the truth before because as I previously said, Bailey was like a brother and I still feared if I did he would come after my family or myself. Bailey was known better by myself than anyone and I knew he had a violent temper. I saw him once previously try to choke another sailor and I honestly thought he would kill him. Many other times I also saw examples of his temper and recall the former Commanding Officer, CDR Bud Orr, USN saying that Bailey was a walking time bomb, after he was confronted about not supporting his wife and his daughter.

"I was aware that Bailey had committed various other rapes in the San Francisco area because he told me about being arrested and put in jail for them prior to entering the navy. This is one reason why I knew when Bailey told me about Jackie, I knew he was telling the truth, and after learning the next day of her murder it became fact.........

"...My last words are that I hope Bailey gets help as I still love him like a brother. I am closer to him than I am to my own family. I decided to tell the truth today because I did not want to see anyone else hurt or killed as a result of Bailey's actions. Also, I could not live with the matter anymore. I have been thinking about her death for almost 2 ½ years since she was murdered by Bailey......The statement is the truth to the best of my knowledge....."

On February 28, 1983, "Smith", after having been advised of his rights and again signing a waiver, submitted to a voluntary polygraph examination to verify his statement. The following relevant questions and responses were noted:

QUESTIONS: RESPONSES:

(A) Were you present when Jackie was killed?   (NO)

(B) Did you cause the death of Jackie?   (NO)

(C) Did you see Jackie in October 1980?   (NO)

I completed the polygraph examination, reviewed the charts and determined there was no deception indicated regarding "Smith's" responses to the relevant questions. He was telling the truth as to Bailey admitting to him he had committed the murder. "Smith" was then returned to NAS Lemoore pending any possible further interviews if needed.

On March 15, 1983, Detective Orth and I drove to the Santa Clara County Jail, San Jose, California, to interview Bailey where he was temporarily being held. We identified ourselves by showing our proper credentials and also advised him of his legal right to have counsel present. Bailey advised he would willingly answer questions and listen to what investigators had to say. During the interview Bailey appeared openly hostile and adamantly denied any involvement in the murder, and even though he was not questioned about the multiple rapes he was being held on, he alluded he was innocent of all those crimes. Even to include the rape where the victim bit off part of his tongue Finally, Bailey stated he would not undergo Polygraph Examination on advice of legal counsel, that he had never "killed anyone", and he wished to return to his cell.

With the sworn statement of "Smith" we were now prepared to arrest Kenneth D. Bailey for the rape/murder of Jackie Wurst. Bailey, by this time was already in Folsom State Prison serving time for previous rapes he had been sentenced to, after having reached an agreement to plead guilty and/or having been convicted. On January 31, 1984, he was then transported and booked into Kings County Jail after having been charged with the homicide/rape (CA Penal Code 187a /190.2a +261a) of HM2 Jacqueline Jane Wurst on October 5, 1980. If convicted on those charges he faced the death penalty or life imprisonment without parole; with special circumstances. It had now been over three years and three months since the crime had been committed and finally the matter was in the hands of the courts.

In March 1984, the Regional Director of Operations for NIS, San Francisco, received a letter from the Sheriff of Kings County, Tom Clark, commending me for "relentlessly and persistently" aiding Detective Orth in the investigation of this case and in succeeding in identifying the suspect. As a result, Detective Orth was able to obtain a complaint and warrant for Kenneth Bailey on the charge of murder. The letter also told of my giving of myself during the investigation and "showing genuine professionalism and expertise."

In July 1984 NIS reassigned me to Europe where I was greatly needed. My wife and I rented out our house, packed all our belongings, took our little dog and flew off to spend the next five years in Europe. With the volume of work I had covering Europe, Africa and the Middle East on that assignment, I had no time to dwell on the Lemoore case or even to follow the trial. It wasn't until much later that I finally learned the outcome of the trial.

CHAPTER 8

DESPITE MANY YEARS OF RAPACIOUS CONDUCT—

Kenneth Duane Bailey was born in Berkeley, California on December 10, 1956, and spent most of his life in the Berkeley/Oakland area prior to joining the Navy. He had family still residing in northern California in later years when he would go on leave from the Navy, which accounted for his repeated trips to the area. At the time of his arrest in Lemoore he was twenty-seven years old, and a strong, six-foot one-inch tall, 180 pound, physically fit young man. I was unable to obtain any information regarding his early family life in my research, only his adult criminal history. But it was well known in later years when ever he was arrested for rape, assault with a deadly weapon, and/or kidnapping the police knew him.

Bailey joined the U.S. Navy around 1978. Court records in Alameda County, his home county, show that from February 1976 to November 1977 he was arrested numerous times for rape, robbery with a weapon, and kidnapping. On February 9, 1976, a twenty-one year old college student was grabbed from behind, overpowered, and raped. On February 22, 1976, another college co-ed was attacked from behind and dragged into a bushy, secluded area where she was sexually assaulted.

On September 27, 1976, while these two cases were pending trial, the defendant, Kenneth Bailey, was free on bail. On that date he was driving a van, later proven to be registered to him, when he opened the passenger door and with a handgun in plain view, ordered his victim into the van. He then drove her to a dark side street, raped her, and then drove her back to the area where he had picked her up, let her out of the van and ordered her not to call the police.

Each of those cases was dismissed, some listed as "in the furtherance of justice" and done so by the prosecutor. Due to various court rulings at the time, such as the "Ballard" ruling, and reluctance of witnesses to testify the prosecution was unable to go on with its case. In "Ballard", the California court had held there may be sexual assault trials in which psychological expert testimony might be admissible to attack the credibility of uncorroborated testimony given by a complainant witness. Under current law this is now disallowed.

October 30, 1977, a college employee working at the campus, was seized from behind by the defendant, dragged into a nearby room and raped. After this he removed $13 from her purse and fled. Bailey was identified in a physical line-up and was charged with her rape and robbery. Bodily fluid samples were obtained from the victim, the crime scene, and the defendant, however forensic analyses were inconclusive and on that basis the case was dismissed.

Since there had been no convictions, Bailey's record was clear and in 1978 he was allowed to join the Navy. Once Bailey joined the Navy and was gone from the Oakland/Berkeley area the series of rapes and assaults ceased, however one does wonder if in the new areas where he was located if he was still active in his crime spree. As best we know, no one ever went back and searched the police records in those other areas to see if he was tied to any crimes committed there. The odds are not in favor of once a criminal is so active he just stops his aberrant behavior, and then acts as a model citizen for three years, only to start up his criminal ways again. Certainly not with the level of violence Bailey showed in his various attacks on women.

We do know, in September 1980, Bailey returned to the United States from an overseas Navy cruise, and was reassigned to a northern California Naval Air Station location. Between then and June 27, 1981, we do not have any public records of any assaults he may have committed. However, on June 27 a fifteen year old was walking home from a bus stop when she was attacked from the rear by Bailey, he put a handgun to her head, grabbed her around the neck, forced her to the ground where he raped her. She promptly reported the attack and was treated at a local hospital.

On August 6, 1981, a young woman was walking to her apartment when she noticed a male following her. As she stepped on to her porch and unlocked her door he grabbed her around the neck from behind and shoved a handgun into her back. She struggled with him and he hit her on the back of the head with his fist then fled the scene. She was not able to identify the assailant from a photograph and was not available to attend a physical line-up. This incident was not held to answer and no evidence was presented at a Preliminary Hearing.

Some twenty-five minutes later a woman was walking on a dark, lightly traveled residential street when she was jumped from behind and groped. At this point she began screaming, the defendant then struck her on the side of the head with a gun and fled on foot. An off duty nurse heard her scream and saw the defendant get into his automobile, and wrote down the license number. This led to his apprehension and identification as the perpetrator of this crime and the one of the fifteen year old also. On August 7, 1981, Bailey was arrested at his residence and the police officers recovered the firearm used in these attacks from the trunk of his car.

Kenneth Bailey was charged in Municipal Court and held to answer for trial in superior court on these two offenses on November 10, 1981. He was released on $10,010 bail and was still awaiting trial on May 11, 1982.

May 11, 1982, was the date of the rape of the college student who had the courage to bite down on the defendants tongue in a manner to rip off the end. Had it not been for her determination to fight off her assailant, regardless of her small body size, and defend herself with all the strength she had, Bailey could have been on the streets once again to continue his violent behavior.

The Pre-sentencing Report and Recommendations by the District Attorney's Office shows that Kenneth Bailey pleaded <u>nolo contendere</u> and was found guilty of the first two attacks. He also pleaded guilty to the third attack. The report described the following:

"CIRCUMSTANCES IN AGGRAVATION;

(a) Facts Relating To The Crimes:
  (1) Each of these offenses involved great violence, the threat of great bodily harm, and other acts disclosing a high degree of cruelty, viciousness and callousness.
  (2) The defendant was armed with and used a handgun. In the other cases discussed above, he also resorted to the use of a gun or knife.
  (3) In each and every instance this defendant attacked solitary women at night, typically in secluded areas where he struck from ambush. Hence each of his victims were particularly vulnerable from the outset. Given his superior size and strength, commonly if not inevitably augmented by weapons, this defendant clearly insisted on picking off the vulnerable.

(4) The defendant has attacked many women.

(5) The manner in which each of the attacks occurred---charged and uncharged--- compels the conclusion that each was premeditated.

(b) Facts Relating To The Defendant:

(1) "This defendant has engaged in a proven pattern of violent, rapacious conduct which indicates an extraordinarily serious danger to society.

(2) "While not previously on probation or parole, the defendant was free on bail when he attacked and raped (victim in September 1977) and (victim in May 1981), awaiting trial on identical charges.

"RECOMMENDATION;

"I respectfully submit that this defendant should be sentenced to state prison for the maximum term permitted by law in punishment for these particularly aggravated and reprehensible attacks.

"This defendant has established himself as a particularly dangerous, callous and persistent rapist over the past several years. He is a walking sex offense looking for a place to happen, and that hazard to the women of this society obtains whether he is free on bail, under investigation, or clear of pending involvement with the criminal justice system.

"The Legislature and the people directly have addressed the danger to society posed by criminals such as this defendant and have given a mandate to the courts to spare society the cancer of their presence.

"Experience has demonstrated that rehabilitation of such felons is a bad joke on the society they victimize repeatedly. In this defendants case the experience has demonstrated that he has previously escaped accountability through his successful manipulation of now defunct previously existing judicially imposed policies which put a premium on legal gamesmanship in the field of criminal procedure to the detriment of the crime victims and society as a whole.

"I respectfully recommend and urge that this defendant be imprisoned for the maximum permissible term in addition to all mandatory enhancements."

The total calculations the King's County District Attorney's Pre-sentencing Report recommended were 708 months—a total of 59 years. This report documents all of the above information. Bailey was given a sentence of twenty-one years by the Court for the rape and assault of eight different women in Alameda County. On December 29, 1982, he arrived at Folsom State Prison, a maximum security facility, to begin his sentence. A prison spokesman speaking to a *Hanford Sentinel* staff writer said Bailey's maximum release date was May 17, 2004; however, he could be eligible for parole in 1997.

In January 1984 Bailey was arrested for the murder of Jacqueline Wurst and in October a preliminary hearing opened to determine if enough evidence existed to bind him over to superior court for trial. At that time he entered a plea of not guilty. The *Hanford Sentinel* reported each court proceeding and their articles showed in November 1984, Bailey's attorneys said the trial would take probably three months and the trial date had been set to begin March 18, 1985. Then because of attorney scheduling conflicts the trial was delayed until September 1985. However, a plea bargain was reached between the prosecutors and Bailey, and in April 1985 Bailey pleaded no contest to a second-degree murder charge and was sentenced to a fifteen-years-to-life term A condition of the plea bargain was struck that Bailey would serve the term concurrent with the twenty-one years sentence he was already serving. In May the parents of Jackie Wurst received a letter from the Kings County Probation Officer to inform them that on May 16, 1985, four years-seven months-and eleven days after their daughter had been murdered, Bailey was finally scheduled to appear for sentencing in Superior Court in Hanford, California. After sentencing, Bailey was returned to Folsom State Prison to continue with his sentence.

CHAPTER 9

AN EXTRA PLOT HAD BEEN LAID ASIDE IN 1859—

On a cool day in October 2005, almost twenty-five years to the day after Jackie was murdered, my wife and I stepped off a plane in Minneapolis, Minnesota, picked up our rental car and headed north to a small town in Wisconsin, across the Upper St. Croix River. After the long flight from California, what with the normal change of planes and slight delays, it was now late evening, dark and hard to follow the hand written directions we had received from Phyllis, Jackie's mother. Nevertheless, we managed to find ourselves in front of the correct hotel in St. Croix Falls, Wisconsin. Jackie had been born in this community on July 16, 1956, and we were now here to meet her parents, Donald and Phyllis Wurst. I had a story to tell them, and they had theirs to pass on to me.

The previous year, the story of Jackie Wurst was still in the back of my mind, as I had always thought of one day writing about her life as a tribute to both she and her family. The stories her friends and co-workers told of her during our investigation of the crime left a tremendous impact on all of us. During my career with NIS I had worked many assault and homicide cases and each one does leave its mark on an investigator but this case was very different. Jackie was from Wisconsin and had that wholesome mid-west upbringing; the same state where I spent my first fifteen years. Jackie had served a Navy tour in Yokosuka, Japan during the same timeframe I had been stationed there. Jackie had been unfortunate and had been sexually assaulted while in Japan but our NIS office was the one which identified who the perpetrator was and was also able to obtain a conviction. Jackie had then later been reassigned to northern California, as I had, and once again NIS was investigating a crime committed against her. This time I was the lucky person to have made the connection to the killer by a simple acronym, "AD2", in a newspaper article I just happened to read.

During the last few years, I had been in contact with Detective Orth on various other matters related to the retirement jobs we both had. One day in one of our conversations I brought up the Wurst case and asked if he had kept in contact with the family and perhaps had a current address for her parents. Larry Orth was very helpful in giving me not only addresses but also furnishing me with copies of newspaper articles and other data that later proved invaluable in writing this book. In October 2004, after all these years, I composed a thoughtful letter to the parents of Jackie. I introduced myself, and told them of my connection to their daughter's murder case and explained what I would like to do, but only with their permission. I mailed the letter, anxiously hoping to hear back in the return mail. Days, weeks, then two months passed, and I began to wonder if I had asked too much of this family. Suddenly after all these years to be asked to open up a terribly deep wound which possibly had managed to fade into the deepest part of their soul, could be more than I, a perfect stranger to them, should ask.

Finally, as Phyllis later explained to me, after much thought, much discussion within their family, and with great apprehension, she made a phone call to me. From the very beginning she was warm and friendly and I soon felt I had known her forever. I then explained to her what I wanted to do, and why, and how I felt deeply this would be something they could be proud of when it was finished. I explained also I didn't just want it to be another murder story, but one which would show how this young woman, in such a short time could make such an impact on so many. She had to have been a very special person, one with a quiet demeanor, compassionate and caring, with extreme loyalty, and always with a wonderful smile. Phyllis then said she and Don were deeply moved by the fact I wanted to tell this story, and they were very willing to help in my endeavor in any way they could. She later said they would love to meet with me and invited my wife and me to visit them in their home.

Now, after all this time, we were finally driving the last twelve miles to the Wurst farm in Osceola. As we went down the country roads, I caught my breath at the beauty of the countryside. Rolling hills, beautifully maintained farms, and the fall colors of the various trees exploding everywhere; the maples were crimson red, the poplars as yellow as the sun on a blazing hot day; the trees were all at their absolute peak of color and it was something I will always remember. Then we passed a county sign which said *"WELCOME, Autumn in Polk County Wisconsin is awaiting you, in its entire splendor."* The brochures Phyllis Wurst had sent us regarding this area stated, *"Come to Polk County just once and you'll be back! Everything from great country hospitality to true northern wilderness are all just a short hour from Minneapolis/St. Paul on the Upper St. Croix River in the Wisconsin glacier region."* All true as we were soon to find out.

Tall yellow poplars lined the road as we approached the farm. The huge blue silos had "Don & Phil Wurst 1968" in big white lettering, and a wooden sign near the mailbox by the roadside said, "Century

Farm, Peter Wurst Homestead since 1859". We knew we had found the right place. We pulled into the driveway which led around to the kitchen door of the old farm house, and Don and Phyllis were there immediately. He grasped my hand in a strong shake; she invited us inside offering coffee and cake. I thought of Jackie, how many people I interviewed had described her as warm and generous, and we followed her parents into their kitchen.

In the large farm kitchen we began to talk of things which were easiest to begin with. My years as an investigator had left in me the simple ability to talk easily with anyone, and to ask any question. I began by asking about the operation of the farm, the number of animals kept, the crops grown, the difficulties farmers have today. I told how my grandfather had been a farmer and how as a young child I had loved going to his farm. Before long Don brought up the event that led to his missing left arm. Don's explanation was one of every farmer's nightmare – his jacket somehow left unbuttoned that day, a manure spreading machine, and the jacket sleeve suddenly caught in the machine. The jacket choking him as the machine pulled it in, and just before he passed out how he managed to call out for help. Son David came running, fortunately with a knife on him, and cut Don free. However, not before the machine had mangled his arm up to the shoulder. Matter-of-factly he described this loss to me.

My daughter likes to say men get along by talking about anything but the thing at hand. "They'll go outside and describe how Mercury and Mars are aligned together this year," she says, "and feel fine." So it was with Don and me. I learned that afternoon when his first ancestor came from Germany, how that great-great Wurst had hewn the barn timbers by hand with a broad axe, how many cows the first son kept, and when the original wooden silo was replaced with concrete. Generation after generation, each Wurst son had built more, repaired the old, upgraded the equipment. Now Jackie's younger brother had made his mark, again hewing from an ash tree a center post to replace the first ancestor's barn work, carving by hand the tongue to fit in the original crossbeam's groove.

Don told us he had been born on the original farm during a blizzard and family lore says that is the reason for his being such a sturdy, hard working man. He is a man with a friendly face and a smile like I envisioned Jackie's to have been; a devoted family man with those mid-west traditions and a strong Christian belief.

Phyllis told us Don was among the first in Northwest Wisconsin to purchase a diesel tractor, bulk milk tank, largest Harvestore for haylage storage and use of liquid manure system. He was also among the first to use herbicides on corn, to use oats as forage, and to raise and harvest three crops in two years. And he was one of the first area farmers to produce Grade A milk. Phyllis also told us in 1975 Don had been nominated by U.S. Public Relations Service, Inc. to appear in the *Who's Who in Wisconsin* for pioneering in modern farming practices. Don went on to tell how in his day of running the farm they used to harvest one hundred bushels of corn per acre, but now with the new technology David is using they reap two hundred bushels per acre. Don is still amazed at what they can produce today with the new genetics and farming practices, and how weed killers can be used to kill off the weeds which take nutrients and water from the soil, yet not harm the crops. We also learned when Don was in High School he was recognized by the *Future Farmers of America* as being first in new farming methods. It is no wonder with this background, both he and David have been such successful farmers.

Don told how he had given up farming in 1987, turning the full operation over to young son David. However, Don, although he claims to be retired, continually assists David in various capacities, some of which are made even more difficult and frustrating because of his previous injury. But there is not a chore to be done, when if needed, he is not out working regardless of the time of day or night. Don's stories filled the day, and I knew this family's strong and complete connection with their land and eighth generation farm.

Phyllis told how she was born in Scandia, Minnesota, just across the river from Osceola. She was of Swedish background and also grew up on a farm, learning to help out as the women do, and also learning to cook those wonderful Swedish dishes. Later we were taken on a drive throughout the area and were able to visit her farm. It is now owned and operated by a new owner but he graciously let us look around.

Eventually Phyllis began to talk of Jackie. A solid farmer like all the Wursts, she grew up with daily chores of feeding the calves, helping to carry the milk, and was also very adept at driving the various machines used to shuck corn and plow the fields. Her strength and athleticism grew from this work until by the time she was in high school, she excelled in track. "She could run like a deer," her mom said, echoing the words of more than one colleague of Jackie's I had interviewed. Throughout these years at home she had a strong interest in and was very active in the 4-H club. This interest allowed her to travel to Kansas, Kentucky, Illinois, Washington D.C. and to Manitoba, Canada.

She also was able to visit France as an intern while in an intercultural program and this enabled her to perfect her French language skills which she had acquired in high school. Phyllis told me Jackie was, like all her children, her class's Valedictorian, and described how she began to love to travel as her 4-H club and French studies took her overseas, and how she eventually wanted to follow her younger sister into nursing. Phyllis added that Jackie's 1974 high school year book reflected about her, "One smile is worth a thousand words," describing the wonderful smile many of her friends had mentioned to me.

After completion of high school in May 1974, Jackie enrolled at the New Richmond Campus in the Nursing Assistant Program where she graduated in May 1975. Upon graduation she went to work at the St. Croix Memorial Hospital as a Nurse's Aid where she remained until she joined the Navy on August 18, 1976. Accomplished, athletic, smart and eager to see the world outside her Wisconsin farm, Jackie joined the Navy to become a hospital corpsman. Jackie reported for active duty on February 23, 1977, and was sent to Florida for Recruit Training where she graduated with distinction and very high test scores, allowing her to be selected to attend U.S. Naval Hospital Corp School, the dream of her life.

The Navy Hospital Corp came into existence June 17, 1898, as an organized unit of the Navy Medical Corps. Its mission was to provide intelligent, capable and efficient assistance to medical and dental officers "in the eternal war against disease, injury and death." Not long after the Corp was established one member was awarded the Congressional Medal of Honor. Hospital Apprentice Robert Standly was cited in 1900 for his exceptionally meritorious conduct in connection with the Allied relief expedition in China during the Boxer Rebellion. During World War I, many members were cited by both the United States and France for Valor and performance of duty under fire. Of the fifteen enlisted men awarded the Medal of Honor in World War II, seven were Navy Hospital Corpsmen. In keeping with tradition, during the Korean conflict five corpsmen were awarded the Medal of Honor.

The life saving services of the hospital corpsmen were called to the front lines again upon the escalation of the Vietnam conflict in 1965. Corp personnel were routinely assigned to the Marine Corps combat units as platoon corpsmen, and would venture out into the dangerous and treacherous jungle with these units to render aid whenever needed. Throughout its history of over one hundred years, the Hospital Corps has successfully fulfilled its mission "to keep as many men, at as many guns, as many days as possible." Wherever you find the Navy or the Marine Corps, the Navy Hospital Corpsman will be there. In times of war, they are on the beaches or in the combat areas with the sailors or marines they serve and attend. They assist in the transportation of wounded by sea and air and serve on all types of ships. In time of peace, they work diligently to maintain the good health and well being of their shipmates. Wherever medical services are required, the Hospital Corpsman is there, willing and ready to serve his country above and beyond the call of duty. This was the military group Jackie had chosen to serve with and was honored to have been accepted into.

"Why do you think Jackie wanted to leave Wisconsin and join the Navy?" I asked Jackie's family.

Her mother answered, "Jackie wanted to follow her sister Charlene into nursing, and her brother Joslyn into the Navy."

"She wanted more in her life," Charlene would later tell me in answer to the same question, "and she liked a challenge."

We sat in the Wurst's comfortable, orderly living room and talked, as the day faded to evening. Phyllis went on to tell us how she had retained almost all of Jackie's belongings including several large boxes of letters she had received from friends of Jackie's, after her death. Having lived in Japan ourselves we noticed items in the home that were obviously mementos from South East Asia. Phyllis told us some of these were gifts from Jackie and some were part of Jackie's household belongings the Navy had returned after her daughter's death. The wooden tray used for cheese and crackers that evening was one Jackie had bought in the Philippines. The china we ate off of during dinner, Jackie had bought in Japan. The curtain hanging over the doorway separating the kitchen from the dining room had been hanging in Jackie's apartment in Japan.

Phyllis uses every item she can which had once belonged to Jackie to keep her memory alive.

Don told us how when the two U.S. Navy personnel, together with the local police, came to the house and informed the family of Jackie's death, he was so traumatized he fell back into a chair and sat unmoving and silent for a full six hours. He said he was totally unable to move or think and just sat there motionless. When he finally was able to look up he saw the Navy personnel were still standing there beside him, just waiting to assist the family in their next step. Finally, he was able to get control of himself and ask them to sit down. He also told of how he had kept all his emotions bottled up inside all these years. He then went on to say how he felt like a huge burden had been lifted from his shoulder after at last being able to talk about this tragedy, especially with someone who could possibly give him the answers he had never received before.

As the day was ending and our first visit was coming to a close, we talked about what we could see and do the following day. Phyllis suggested perhaps in the afternoon we might go to the cemetery which was located just a short distance from the farm. She said all of the Wurst family is buried there, going back to the first generation to arrive in the area. She then went on to say how when she and Don had gone to the cemetery to arrange for a burial plot for Jackie they were told a very bizarre fact. They were informed three grave plots had been laid aside in the original Wurst homestead grant, dating back to 1859, and no one in the family ever knew this before. The plots were now turned over to Don, Phyllis and their Jackie. What a strange coincidence an extra plot was made available way back then, one which now allowed Jackie to be buried next to where her parents will eventually be laid to rest.

CHAPTER 10

JACKIE, JACKIE, WHY DID THEY DO
THIS TO YOU?

Wurst family homestead, since 1859, Osceola, WI

The next morning when we returned to the farm, Jackie's sister Charlene was there. Our first impression was of an emotionally strong individual, a Wurst characteristic we would eventually see in each family member we met. Charlene was also reticent to talk to us and we sensed she had many questions regarding why I wanted to write this story. It had been twenty-five years and why now would someone be so interested in their family? What was I going to gain by prying into a tragedy they had all managed to put far into the recesses of their minds? She also was afraid we would end up putting Jackie on a pedestal because of what happened to her, when she had only been a normal person. Fortunately, I was able to use my talent for talking to anyone to open a conversation with her. Soon she was as warm and friendly as her parents and began to tell us about her childhood days with Jackie.

Wurst family home in Osceola, WI

Charlene was fifteen months younger than her sister and the two girls were very close. They shared the same bedroom, would wear each others clothes, worked together doing their assigned household chores and shared childhood secrets. Charlene told us she remembered the "inch me, pinch me" they did in bed to make sure they each stayed on their own half of the bed. They would spend hours playing with their dolls, making houses with a blanket and chairs. The summers were spent outside with the animals as they treated them like they were kids, making braided twine halters for the calves to lead them around. She also said, "To this day I cannot imagine what we were thinking when we would call dibs on who helped with the evening milking and who would do the dishes. Dishes took forty-five minutes where the stint in the barn was three hours. In the summer it was hot and you got to put up with the flies and switching cow tails but we both really enjoyed being in the barn."

Antique Wurst family photograph, Osceola, WI

Charlene went on to say, "I've always wondered how much of a role our siblings play in our personalities. Because Jackie was as quiet as she was, I was the one who drove us everywhere, got directions, and had to ask the questions. That changed briefly when she was home to pack before leaving for Japan. She actually drove to Fort Snelling to drop off her trunk but then she made me drive to the Minnesota State Fair from there. Don't remember if I told you we were planning on living together when she got out of the service. She was studying for the LVN boards and planned on going to school to be an RN. As far as music goes, we didn't have disposable money growing up so the music she bought was when she was in the service. That was the days of John Denver and Gordon Lightfoot. I do remember driving back to the hospital before her funeral and hearing an Anne Murray song, *Could I Have This Dance.* I remember crying through the whole thing and to this day can't hear the song without it taking me back to those days around the funeral."

Photograph of Wurst original farm property

Charlene told us about her husband and three nearly grown boys, who it seems, have the same strong work ethic and personality. She said, "Neither my husband, Dan, nor the boys ever met Jackie yet the two oldest, John and Ben, would talk about her like they were friends. I've always had a picture of her in my bedroom and they have known who she is but they would know things about her I had never told them. Our youngest son, Matt, was a risk taker. No piece of furniture was high enough to not be conquered or low enough to not be jumped off of. Can't tell you how many times we "lost" him either. Both Dan and

I always said Matt had a host of guardian angels keeping him safe and we know whose special project he was. We don't sense her in our lives so much any more but we still know she is around. Find a penny and it is an instant reminder of her." She also told how she had finished her nurses training years before and now worked as a Registered Nurse in a local hospital. Listening to her and watching her demeanor, I could tell she was smart and sharp, and I sensed she was probably an efficient and caring nurse. Later, Phyllis confirmed what I thought.

Photograph of original deed to Wurst property dated 1859

At one point in our conversation with the family, I suddenly realized I didn't know if anyone was aware of the assault on Jackie when she was stationed in Japan. I stopped in the middle of my sentence and asked Charlene to step outside with me. I thought if anyone would know she probably was the one. Jackie might have confided in her. But still I had to be careful in case no one knew. Outside, I asked her if Jackie had said anything about a problem she had while in Japan and she said, "Yes". From the way she answered, I knew she was fully aware of the incident.

Aerial view of Donald and Phyllis Wurst farm, Osceola, WI

Later in the day she went into more of an explanation as to how she found out. She said in the Wurst home when ever a letter from Jackie would arrive, the person whose name was on the outside of the envelope was the one allowed to open it. But from then on the letter became "public information" and was read to everyone. This particular day Charlene opened the letter addressed to her, and was ready to read aloud when the first sentence said, "Please do not read this to Mom and Dad." Jackie then went on in the letter to say she had been assaulted while asleep in her barracks but she was okay and would get over it. She just didn't want her parents to know what had happened as it would upset them. Somehow Charlene managed to quickly skip that part of the letter and finish reading the rest, get out of the room and hide the letter – hoping the family would not ask to read it again. In one of our private conversations with Phyllis she told us she had found out by accident from one of Jackie's close friends and had then told Don; always keeping it quiet from the rest of the family.

After lunch we all drove the short distance to the Oak Grove Cemetery in Farmington, the next town over, and there we were shown the Wurst family section. The cemetery is located just across the street from the church where all the Wurst family worshiped, and where the funeral for Jackie was held. All the ancestors are buried there and right in line is the large stone now designated for Don, Phyllis and Jackie: those three grave sites assigned so many years ago. Also, there is a white marble head stone provided by the Veteran's Administration with Jackie's name, military rate, date of birth and death. A beautiful, simple, but very moving tribute to one of our young military personnel.

Wurst family cemetery monument Farmington, WI

Afterwards, Charlene made arrangements for us to go to the home of David, the youngest of the five children of Don and Phyllis. When David took over the operation of the farm, Don and Phyllis moved into a smaller house on the adjacent acreage and let David and his wife and two children live in the original Wurst home. This was the home where they had all grown up, had the original barn, and had so many memories of Jackie. It is a large home with a screened porch across the whole front, with the living room, dining room, and parent's bedroom downstairs and large bedrooms upstairs for the children. There is a large farm style kitchen with a mudroom entrance which everyone uses rather than the front door. Outside the kitchen, just a short distance away is the family vegetable garden. Close at hand, easy to get to when preparing meals.

We were introduced to David and Beth, his wife. Beth had been a school teacher in Milwaukee, Wisconsin, when she met David and moved to the farm after they were married. Don describes them as a team equal to none when it comes to farming and says Beth has taken to it as though she had been born into farming. They of course had plenty of work to be done during our day with them, but they did their best to explain the operations of a dairy farm to my wife, who is a pure Californian; one who only knows big cities, sunshine and beaches. They showed us the old barn and where the restoration work was done. David at the age of fourteen cut an ash tree from the woods to make a new center post on the south side, complete with tongue to fit the slot in the original cross beam. David has continually maintained the barn, replacing side walls and bad posts, building a new feed manger, even having the barn repainted for the first time in almost one hundred years. He told us the barn had been continuously used to house cattle for nearly one hundred-fifty years and that now it is used to store baled hay, machinery, seed and as a home to a dozen or so chickens.

That evening while sitting and talking we learned the history of the barn, and David gave us a copy of an article he had written regarding the barn. It is one of the oldest barns in the Osceola area and was most likely built around 1860, when Martin Wurst first arrived in the United States. His brother Peter had the adjoining farm (where Don and Phyllis now live) but he had been killed during the Civil War and the property then added to Martin's farm. We were told the barn is unique because its beams and frame were hand sawn with a broad axe instead of being sawed at a saw mill as later barns were done. The men on the farm spent the winter months in the woods chopping each beam for a specific purpose and the beams were then fitted together by inserting tongues (narrow squared ends) into slots or notches in other beams. Wooden dowel pins held the joints together. The barn is a single story with a dirt floor, and in one side horses and cows were kept, and in the other side hay and machinery was stored. Additional hay was stored in the loft above the animals.

After a bit, David asked me to step into the kitchen area with him, away from the wives and his children, as there were questions he wanted to ask regarding Jackie's death. At the time of her death he was only eleven years old and wasn't told any of the horrible details. Through the years, as he matured, he learned more of what had happened to his sister but he was never sure if he was really given all the details. I answered his questions and told him details of the investigation. Somewhere, he had even heard of the incident in Japan and I answered his questions regarding that as well. Then I asked if he had many memories of his sister. Since he was only eight years old when she went away to boot camp, and being much younger than she, he was not too much aware of what all she did.

The one memory he had which has always stayed with him though, was after her death, the day Jackie's personal belonging's arrived. The Navy had all her belongings packed and shipped to her parents who were still living in the big house. Don, when the truck arrived, was out working on the farm and it was left to Phyllis to accept the shipment. The delivery truck men unloaded everything and placed it all on the big, front screened porch with Phyllis standing by. David being unsure of what was going on went off into another part of the house. It wasn't long after the men had left when he heard someone talking and crying and he still was unsure of what was going on. He remembers peeking around the door and seeing his mother going through the boxes and furniture, crying and talking to Jackie and as she did so saying, "Jackie, Jackie, why did they do this to you?" It was a long time before he could go outside to sit with his mother. Even as a young child he knew she needed to be alone at that moment.

Jackie after completing Boot Camp on her way to Corp school in Great Lake, IL

During the evening the oldest son, Joslyn, came in to meet us. He also lives on a farm just across the road from the family home. Joslyn, like his siblings, had been an A student in school and after graduation in 1973, had joined the Navy. After completion of boot camp his academic and aptitude scores were high enough that it was determined he would be sent to a service school to learn the mechanics of how to repair Navy equipment. There he excelled in the training, graduated early and was promoted to the Engineman Rate. His promotions were rapid and he soon was promoted up the ranks to Engineman Second Class, EN2. After fixing old tractors, trucks, manure spreaders, harvesters and any other piece of equipment on the farm, this new line of work was easy for him. He remained in the Navy for four years, served on two Navy vessels, distinguished himself, and just before leaving the service passed the examination for Petty Officer First Class. A remarkable achievement, but again a common fact of life in the Wurst family.

Joslyn, like Charlene, had many questions as to why I wanted to write this story. His first reaction was why would anyone care after all these years? He also had his questions to be answered regarding the investigation, but his having been in the Navy made it easier for him to understand how NIS worked. I liked this young man and could relate easily to him due to my previous Navy background, and continue to correspond with him to this date, as we each find time.

The only member of the Wurst family I was not able to meet on this trip was the youngest sister Faith. Faith and her family currently live in Florida and in later communications she told me of her memories of Jackie. To me they are so poignant I don't want to summarize them, therefore with your permission, Faith, I am writing them verbatim.

Faith starts:

"Here goes:

"My memories of Jackie are few simply because I was so young. I do remember playing ball (softball that is) out on the yard in front of the granary. That was something that we all did as a family, but I have no specific memory involving Jackie.

"As younger sister I looked up to my older siblings (and most likely drove them insane). I recall that Jackie spent time with me teaching me manners---whether it was table manners or in my relations with other people. We both had/have a lot of hair on our arms (at least for girls).

I recall the time she talked with me about training it to lay down so that it was not fly-away. She said that after I take my shower I should rub it in one direction going around my arm so that it does not stick up. I do think this is a very strange thing to remember, but it really worked. It made the abundance of hair on my arms less noticeable which was good because I was/am a very self conscience person. I think the reason I was so accepting to Jackie's advice/help/suggestions (I am very independent and always want to do *my* thing) was her kind, gentle way of imparting knowledge---not bossy. I don't remember any other specific instances of her manner training of me, but I do know that she worked with me a lot. I believe that I sat next to her at the dinner table.

"Jackie was in 4-H and she often made things for me for 4-H projects. She made clothes and even made a bedspread with matching curtains (which I still have by the way) when my room was repainted. The material has kittens on it.

"For my confirmation I received a cross necklace with an opal in it. She also bought me a jacket (I think from Korea) and a dress from the Philippines (which I wore at her funeral).

"I recall that Mom & Dad had her purchase china for both Char & I when she was in Japan. I received that when Rich & I got married, which, even though she didn't actually pay for it, she still had her part in it. I do think of her when I use it even though it was really from Mom & Dad.

"Unfortunately many of my memories and thoughts related to Jackie are connected with her death. I was in high school at a prep school at the time of her death. I was pulled out of class and had to go see the dorm mother. That was stressful enough--wondering what I had done wrong that got me in that much trouble. The memory of being told that she had been killed has faded with time, but is still quite fresh in my mind. This may be more of a therapy session rather than what information you are really looking for! I took my first airplane ride in a four or six seater plane to get home to be with my family. When we realized it could be awhile before the funeral I was flown back to Prairie du Chien, Wisconsin. Only to turn around a few days later and fly back up for the funeral. I remember viewing the casket which was very important I believed that I do. However, despite seeing her in the casket, I went through a *long* time of thinking that it wasn't really her there. That it was a mistake and that it was someone else that 'they' thought was her and that she was really alive. There are obvious holes in that story so I would sometimes take it further with she was hiding out from everyone (for who knows what reason I concocted!) That was better for me than believing that she was dead. I know that there were times years later when I would think that I saw her and would have to remind myself of reality—she was dead.

"After the funeral, Mom and Dad drove me back to school. Here is another very strange thing that is like yesterday to me (don't ask me why). Dad got stopped for speeding (I could show you the general location unless they have changed the road too much.) He explained what the situation was (that they were taking me back to school after Jackie's funeral). I can still see the officer looking at me in the back seat right behind Dad and asking me if he should let him go this time (I don't think that Dad was ever stopped for speeding before or since). What was I to do (with my bleary eyes about ready to cry again) but shake my head "yes" which of course he did. (I don't know if I'm divulging some great secret with that story!!!)

"After that I know that I struggled with Jackie's death in a variety of ways. I am very thankful that I was in the school that I was in to have answers to my unending questions. Every day we had a devotion in the chapel on the campus. One day one of the professors spent the entire devotion time with me as I was trying to deal with Jackie's death. There was another professor who frequently got questions from me. One of the things I struggled with was the thought that Jackie was watching me all the time. (I wonder as I write this if I was trying to make her into God!!) He reassured me that since in heaven we are never sad, she couldn't be watching me because of the fact that my concern dealt with the fact that she would see me do things that were wrong which, of course, would not make her happy.

"The other thing that I had to learn to deal with was being called Jackie. I looked a lot like Jackie and some of my relatives called me Jackie from time to time. My normal reaction is to say nothing at all which is what I did. Even though the first time it happened it kinda stopped me in my tracks. It actually happened often enough that I just let it slide and went about as though it had not happened.

"I definitely have missed Jackie over the years and now that I have gotten older I wonder what my life would be like if my *other* sister was alive and what she would be like. Things like weddings and family gatherings and visits.

"I guess that brings up another situation that I never have come up with a way to handle. The inevitable question: so how many brothers and sisters do you have (or some rendition of it). I *always* hesitate and evaluate before I answer. Do I want to get into the fact that Jackie was killed, or not? How I present the information determines where the conversation goes."

CHAPTER 11

—AND STILL THOSE BOXES OF CARDS AND LETTERS

Another day on the farm and we are now beginning to feel as though we have some insight into this Wurst family. We have met the parents, the two brothers and one sister of Jackie's who live in the area. We have seen the town of Osceola and know where Jackie went to school, where she received her education and excelled in track, although it is now a new school, not the same as before. We have been shown the surrounding countryside; have seen where her aunts and uncles lived, where her mother grew up. We have seen the complete workings of the farm and the dairy cattle, and the acres and acres of corn and soy beans ready for harvesting. We watched David and Beth do their chores and saw how David had set up a hand operated corn shucker for his young son to use for corn to feed the chickens. A similar one had been there for David when he was a youngster and had that same chore and now his son, the eighth generation to walk through the barn, was doing the same thing. We have talked until late at night with this family as they opened up to us and expressed their sorrows and also told of many happy days. We now can truly understand where Jackie's strong sense of moral values, her loyalty to family and friends, and her warmth and compassion came from. And also why she always had such a wonderful smile on her face. This is a remarkable family.

This day we were told by Phyllis she would show us the boxes of old photos she had in case there were any we wanted to copy. She had every photo Jackie had sent home very neatly placed into albums; each telling a story of where Jackie had traveled, her friends, and where she had lived. This we could tell was not easy for Phyllis and Don, bringing up such painful memories. But they never paused and said, "No more". We saw all the albums and the many certificates of achievement Jackie had received. Then Phyllis said there are still several boxes of cards and letters received after Jackie's death. After the family had read them all Phyllis had bundled everything together in neat stacks and packed it all away in several very large cartons. When asked, she said she guessed there were probably four hundred to five hundred pieces of mail.

Phyllis gently opened the boxes and started separating the stacks. There were sympathy cards, most of which had at least a short personal note, and there were letters, all handwritten. Some were from relatives, some were from close friends, and also a great number were from people who said they didn't know Jackie well, but just wanted the family to know what a beautiful young woman she was and how sorry they were. Each piece of mail conveyed the same sympathetic message, expressed in the most individual way of the writer. Some had obviously been written with great difficulty as the person tried to express his sorrow and also his shock at what had happened. And each and every one of these cards and letters had been answered with the date noted; we can only imagine how difficult a task this was under the circumstances.

As we read through a selection of these letters, Phyllis told us how two of Jackie's closest friends had constantly, through all these years, maintained contact with her—never missing a Christmas or the anniversary of Jackie's death. In fact, when we arrived there was a beautiful arrangement of flowers on the table which Marilyn had just sent. Marilyn (Lang) Williams and Chris Appel had both known her since boot camp in Florida. Later all three had been transferred to Japan to work in the hospital in Yokosuka. Marilyn, at one point, had been Jackie's roommate in Japan and later had been reassigned to Northern California, however a different hospital than Jackie.

We found a letter from OJ, the last person known to have seen her alive, other than the killer, written just five days after her death. A very poignant letter, telling the family how he worked with Jackie and had trained her as his relief at the ER check-in desk. How they had spent many happy hours in conversation and were close friends. And how even the day when she had a problem with her car, she maintained her usual positive and pleasant outlook and just wanted to go ride her bike and study. He went on to say how personnel at the base had taken a collection and were in the process of deciding on an appropriate memorial for Jackie and he would keep the family informed. OJ wrote a number of letters to the family for several years, each one expressing how he still thought of Jackie and missed her, and how hard it still was for him to deal with the tragedy.

In the midst of reading letters and cards Phyllis remembered certain comments which had really touched her. She remembered being asked by a senior officer at Lemoore, what he should do with the potted plants Jackie had. When she told him to just give them away he said he would have a problem as there were 192 people who wanted them as a memory of Jackie. She also remembered being told an Asian lady who lived in the apartment below Jackie's kept calling the base for information. She said Jackie had been helping to teach her children English and they missed her so much.

There were letters from patients who told how friendly and efficient Jackie was. There was a letter from Don and Phyllis's local bank manager commending them for the example they set in their community and for the strength of character they displayed under such an immensely difficult situation. There was a letter from a young couple who had known Jackie and worked with her at the Naval Hospital in Japan, and had witnessed Jackie's kindness and love for her patients and how gentle and serene she was. Also, a second letter from another young couple in Japan said Jackie used to baby sit for them, and they would sit and talk about Wisconsin with her as they were also from there.

Then there was the letter from a young woman who knew Jackie from playing softball on the base softball team. She told how just two weeks previously she had the chance to discuss with Jackie their future plans after their enlistments. She said Jackie told her "I plan on going to school to become an RN after completion of the Navy. I'm going to allow my parents to retire early --- I love my parents very much!" Then the young woman went on to say how she hoped "to follow in Jackie's footsteps as she seemed to have her head together—her values and goals were organized and realistic."

Many, many letters---each sharing the writer's grief and trying to give some comforting word to Jackie's parents. They all told of the high moral character of Jackie, her kindness and her willingness to help anyone who was feeling sad or troubled. How she wore her uniform with great pride and was always immaculate in her appearance; a wonderful example to all who knew her. Some of the letters contained photos the writers had of Jackie which they thought the parents would love to have.

Perhaps the most poignant of all though, was the letter from Doctor Fred Riegel, M.D., who delivered Jackie when she was born. He told of the shock of reading the account in the newspaper and then remembering the "bouncing baby girl of some twenty-four years ago." He told of her being such a great nurse's aide when she worked at the

St. Croix Falls Hospital, and how often when he would see her in the hallway he would nudge one of his fellow doctors and say "there goes one of my babies." He went on to say how many at the hospital were pained by the senseless loss and would not forget easily.

All of these letters and cards, each one filled with grief, had been neatly packed away. Each message, in its' own individual way, trying to convey to Jackie's family the sympathy felt by all. These treasured remembrances of their daughter which Don and Phyllis have saved all these years and as they said, they will never destroy.

CHAPTER 12

THE YELLOW BIKE FROM THE CRIME SCENE—

One of the letters we read, written in January 1981, told how hospital personnel wanted to establish a memorial tribute to Jackie. It had finally been decided they would place a plaque in the dining hall since it was used mostly by hospital staff, and it could then be their private tribute to her. The plaque was made with Jackie's photo and an inscription which detailed her life in the Navy. It told of her various assignment locations, how she excelled in her off-duty endeavors and had been named the Overall Female Athlete of the Air Station for the fourth quarter of 1980. It went on to say how she gave of her own time to help educate foreign children in the English language within her apartment complex. And then closed with, "This dining room has been dedicated as a Memorial tribute to Jackie for it was here that as the Collection Agent we all came to know her for her delightful personality which inspired us all."

We were nearing the end of our time with Don and Phyllis and their family. Although we had been given complete access to all the letters, cards, and photos, had been allowed to copy any of the items, and had heard many stories from the family, we still found each answer led us to another question. Phyllis thought perhaps we would like to personally talk with Jackie's closest friends. She suggested we contact both Marilyn Williams and Chris Appel, the two women who still maintained contact with her. We took down their addresses and assured her we would contact them as soon as we returned home. She was confident they would be willing to share their memories of Jackie with us.

Jackie's yellow bike at crime scene on October 6, 1980

As we were discussing who else we could contact, we suddenly became aware that several times while we had been looking at photos Phyllis had quietly mentioned we should find "Carl". She showed us photos of him and Jackie taken in Yosemite, that beautiful nature spot located in central California, and I had even commented on one particular photo. It was a close-up of Jackie with the high mountains of Yosemite in the background with almost a surreal look to it. Don spoke up and said it was also his favorite photo of his daughter. Carl, we were told, had been a good friend of Jackie's when they were both stationed in Japan, and since we didn't have a "boyfriend" to contact we took down his name. Unfortunately, Phyllis didn't have a current address for him—only his father's address which was now more than twenty-five years old. Jackie had always been very private about her boyfriends, and as we later learned, many of the young men who knew her wished they could have had a closer friendship. She was just the perfect girl you would like to take home to "mom".

Later in the day, we asked if we could go back over to David's farm one last time. We had enjoyed our first day there and wanted to be sure and say our goodbyes to David and Beth, and take one last walk through the area. David graciously stopped his work to join us and suddenly stooped over and picked up a small, very colorful, Sebright bantam rooster we were told was named "Cyril". Cyril was as tame as the rest of the farm animals and had been taught to do a nice "cock-a-doodle-doo" on command. David spoke to Cyril and told him to "Say hello to Tom" and Cyril threw back his head, pushed out his chest, ruffled up his feathers and did his cock-a-doodle-do. He was then told to "Say hello to Bev" and again he performed his trick. Phyllis much later told me she had taken a photo of Cyril and me at the time, and had entered it in the Osceola Fair and had won a red ribbon, the first time she had ever entered photos in the Fair.

Being a large farm with a good size herd of dairy cattle there was also Johnny the dog. Johnny was a rather old, brown and white sheep dog and was missing one ear and had many a scar, mostly from his entanglements with the raccoons. David told of one particular episode where Johnny chased a raccoon and it jumped on his ear and hung on---with Johnny running in circles trying to fling it off. After that Johnny was really after the 'coons and would sit at the base of a tree howling until the farmers came and took them out. Johnny's main job though, was to herd the cows. As we were talking to Cyril, David noticed one of the cows had left the milking barn and was wandering out into the open area. David yelled to Johnny, "get the cows!" and off went Johnny---barking at the heels of the cow to herd it back into the barn. Once the cow was back inside and at his proper milking station, David told Johnny to "be nice" which meant not to bite the cow and his job was done.

As dinner time approached, we had to leave the farm for the last time, and while we were still standing and talking with Phyllis and Don, we looked up and the younger Wurst group was heading into their house. First in line was David, the big, strong, head of the farm; next came Beth, the wife, mother and former school teacher turned farmer; third in line was young Michael, the eighth generation young farmer whose job was to feed the chickens; behind Michael was Katie, small and just past toddler stage; these all were followed by Johnny the dog, papa cat, momma cat, five little kittens one by one, and last of all was Cyril the rooster. This long line of the Wurst family spread out half way across the yard between barn and house, and not one of them realized the lasting image they projected. It was just time to go in for dinner and one by one they went, the family inside the house and the animals waiting on the porch. My camera went up but there was no way to capture the whole procession in one clip. It was one of those moments when one has to rely on memory, and which I will always remember each time I think of the last day on the farm.

Earlier on the way to the farm, I happened to remember the bike of Jackie's which she had ridden out to the Marina that fateful day. I asked Don and Phyllis if they ever got it back from the Navy since it had been retained as part of the crime scene evidence. They said it had finally been returned with the other items which had also been held. When we arrived at the old barn Phyllis and Don stepped inside and motioned to just inside the door. There on the right against the wall, where it had been placed many years ago was the yellow ten-speed bike. The one we recognized from the crime scene photos, now covered with a thick layer of dust and with the seat slowly disintegrating. It was as though no one had dared to move it until this moment, when they gently brought it out for us to see and photograph. After which, it was just as gently returned to its spot in the old barn. It was apparent to us all things connected to Jackie were treated with this great love and sorrow, and we knew it would be our challenge to continue doing the same in this story of her gentle soul.

As this day was ending, so was our visit with the Wurst family. We had arrived filled with trepidation, and they had greeted us not knowing what to expect or really what we wanted. Now we felt a closeness to each of them as we had been allowed to enter into their private lives. We were fully aware it had not been an easy thing for them to open up to us, and after many years discuss a very private family tragedy. Our one hope was that we were not leaving them with a huge open wound which would again take many years to heal. That was the main question we asked as we said those goodbyes. "Was it wrong of us to ask so much of them?" Phyllis assured us we had been gentle in our approach and not too inquisitive, too fast---giving them time to think through their feelings and answers. When we told Don how we hoped we had not been too invasive and caused too much pain, his answer was remarkable. He said he had not felt this good in the past twenty-five years; it was a huge relief for him to at last been able to talk about the tragedy, something he had just buried deep inside of himself. And finally, he said, after all this time he had his first night of uninterrupted sleep.

Chapter 13
The dead Cottonwood tree
below the knoll—

As we were flying home on the long plane ride, we had plenty of time to reflect back on our many conversations of the past week. We felt we had been fortunate to have been invited into this private world of the Wurst family. Not only had we been allowed into their homes but they had been gracious, open with their feelings and emotions, and willing to share their memories of their daughter who had been taken from them in such a vicious way. We also had plenty of happy times to remember— like the day David took me out on the combine, one of the largest made today and even let me have a turn at driving, as he harvested those acres and acres of corn. We thought of the superb dinners prepared by Phyllis, a fabulous Swedish cook, and how fresh the food had been, all grown in the family garden. We remembered the vivid fall colors as we made the drive into Osceola and surrounding countryside, how absolutely brilliant with color the leaves were at their peak. It was an experience we both will never forget. But now we needed to move on and start trying to locate Jackie's friends and co-workers from twenty-five years ago, with the hope of getting their memories of time spent with Jackie.

I started this new task by writing letters to the old addresses I had taken off the many cards and letters which Phyllis had saved. I also had the current addresses of both Marilyn and Chris, Jackie's former roommates, and I sent letters to them. I had also found a recent letter, though still four years old, from a Jim Ashley who had been with Jackie in Japan. He had not found out about her death until sometime in 1982, because of his having been transferred to other areas. That year he had made contact with a former, mutual co-worker who informed him of the murder. Then in 2001, while doing a genealogy research on various relatives and friends, he came across the notice of Jackie's death. He then decided to write to the Wursts to learn the final outcome as to whether the murderer had ever been caught. My hope was, with these few current addresses I could make contacts which would possibly lead me on to others who had known Jackie, and could provide me with more information. Again, I realized that a letter coming out of the blue regarding this horrific incident could be shocking to some of her close friends, and I knew I had to be quite careful in my approach. I mailed all my letters hoping to hear back soon, but as often happens, other priorities in peoples lives seemed to take precedent, and I waited and waited for answers. Many of the letters came back marked "unknown, undeliverable", and many were not even returned, probably just thrown out by current occupants—not wholly unexpected after all these years.

The one person, Jim Ashley, whom I thought would be easy to locate because his address was more recent and fairly close to where I was living at the time, proved to be not quite so easy. I made phone calls to a number listed for his address but never received call backs, and mail sent to the address was also returned. Finally, after a great deal of effort was expended I decided to just take a ride and try to find his house, and see if a neighbor might have information. Old fashioned legwork turned out to be what was needed. I was told he had moved the year before to the state of Washington and was living with his mother. With that information I was able to get a telephone number for contact. Jim Ashley quickly responded to my message and told how he was one of Jackie's many admirers who had a crush on her, although he never actually dated her. He talked a lot about how they worked together on the night shift at the hospital in Japan and how conscientious Jackie was in her duties. He also explained while doing his genealogy research he had found the name "David Wurst" and had sent his inquiring letter. Phyllis had answered the letter, as she had done each piece of correspondence received, and had given him the update on the case.

While waiting for letters to come back I called Larry Orth, the Detective who had worked the case and who is now retired, and in our conversation asked him if he would be willing to return to the crime scene with me. He agreed and we set a date. We met at a local restaurant and discussed where the area was, how we would get there, and he then told me the Marina area was no longer in use by anyone. We talked of how the area had been at the time of the crime, how there was a hard-packed dirt road going in but easy to maneuver, and how lush and green the grasses and trees were. How full the river was, and how all the tributaries flowed into the coves and around the small islands the various higher elevations made. How the people used to bring their boats and just push them down a short way into the water, and how the swimmers could jump off the edge and not get hurt since the water was deep enough. The aerial photos taken after the crime showed what a beautiful location this was, and it didn't take any imagination to understand why people loved it.

The area turned out to be not too far from the back gate of the Lemoore Naval Air Station, an easy drive to the cut-off road. Then we started down a hard, dried-mud-packed, rutted road, which obviously had not been used in years. Weeds had grown up in the ruts; trash had been dumped in those years and was blown around everywhere. Old rubber tires and dead car batteries were strewn about. The further we drove the deeper the ruts and harder the road was to navigate, to the point we almost turned back, but our four-wheel drive vehicle plus our persistence in hoping to reach the final spot, made us push on. We couldn't see any river or water at all and I kept wondering when we would finally reach the Kings River.

Detective Larry Orth, (Ret) and Special Agent Brannon, NCIS, (Ret),
at crime scene twenty-five years later

Soon we reached the absolute end of the drivable part of the rutted road, and just left our car and walked the last one hundred feet or so. Sure enough, there was the knoll but now covered in thick, dead weeds. And there was the Cottonwood tree just below the knoll, but now totally dead, with its main branches broken off and just piled onto the weeds where they fell. Then we saw the spot where Jackie had been found floating face down in the water, but now empty of any water. The tributaries that had flowed off from the Kings River and which had formed so many great swimming holes and coves were now completely dried up. Off in the distance we could see the river but this whole area was now just a desolate, overgrown, weedy, trash strewn, dried up spot.

Looking at the place, I couldn't imagine I was in the former Marina where so many of the military and local residents had spent those peaceful days, enjoying the coolness of water in the hot summers, and the warm fall days. I was there at the same time of year as when the murder had happened, and yet the vegetation and landscape was like it was from another planet. It brought to my mind the interviews of base personnel shortly after the murder, when many had said they would never go out to the Marina again, and now I could see everyone had abandoned it. To me, at that moment, it seemed as though even God had abandoned the area.

CHAPTER 14
SHE QUIETLY AND GENTLY TOUCHED YOUR LIFE—

In one of my conversations with Larry Orth I had asked about the other investigator on the case, Darryl Henry. Larry gave me his number to call and Darryl quickly responded to my message. He said he vividly recalled the case and how thorough the investigation was conducted and also how frustrating it was as well. He said he had never worked any other investigation which had as many leads that ran you into a brick wall.

Detective Henry, like others involved in the case became emotionally attached as he learned the history of the victim, Jackie Wurst. He was born and raised in southern Minnesota and was aware of the high values held by most Midwestern farm families. He said Jackie fit the mold of a Midwestern farm girl with her high values and morals. Darryl had also spent eleven years in the Navy prior to joining the Kings County Sheriff's Office and felt an attachment to the Navy personnel at the Lemoore Air Station.

Darryl remembered and remarked how after the case went cold for over two years, the break finally came when I read the acronym AD2 in the San Francisco newspaper. He also commented how if I had not made the connection chances are the case would never have been solved. March 4, 1983, after the suspect was apprehended, Detective Henry and Detective Orth contacted Bailey at the Santa Clara County jail where he was in custody for another sexual assault. Henry said Bailey had denied killing Jackie, however, also denied raping the coed who had bit off part of his tongue during a rape, so they believed his credibility was lacking. Detective Henry added in March 1984 they learned from the State Crime Laboratory that Kenneth Bailey's blood type was consistent with some evidence found at the crime scene. Today, with DNA, the evidence would be more conclusive.

Darryl said he had never returned to the murder scene but in his normal driving routine he often drives the main highway nearby, and he always thinks of the victim and the terrible crime committed there. After my phone call to him he said he immediately drove out to the exact location and also felt like "God had abandoned the location", noting how desolate and eerie it is now.

Detective Darryl Henry remained with the Kings County Sheriff's Office, attaining Sergeant, Lieutenant and Captain's rank until his retirement in August 1996. He currently teaches Law Enforcement discipline courses at a local college in Kings County.

Also while talking with Larry Orth, I asked if he had kept in contact with any of the Navy people who were at Lemoore in 1980, or knew where any of them were now located, as he still lives in the area. He told me that Doctor Willie Ewing, M.D., was in private practice locally and gave me the phone number where he could be reached. Dr. Ewing had left the Navy after about eleven years and had gone on to a very successful private practice and where he remains today. In later years I talked with many people in the area and they all either knew him or knew of him, and all spoke highly of Dr. Ewing.

When I called Dr. Ewing I explained who I was and why I was calling and asked if he remembered Jackie Wurst. He replied it was something he has thought of often and would never forget. He went on to say when she had been found he was the one who had pulled her body from the water and had pronounced her dead. He also said he had known her personally and she was a dedicated, caring person and without a doubt was one of the best liked persons in his command, and this fact made it difficult to understand why someone would kill her. Then he went on to tell how when she failed to show up for work he feared something was wrong as it was not in her nature to be late, and how the next day they had formed the search team which eventually led to finding her.

Since few of my letters had produced any possible interviews, I decided I needed more help in locating individuals. I called an old friend and former NIS Special Agent, now retired and operating his own Private Investigative business. Ron Janson spent more than twenty years as a Special Agent, and prior to that had been a police officer with the Santa Barbara, California Police Department for ten years. During his time with our organization, he had multiple assignments throughout the United States and overseas. He was an extremely tenacious and hard working individual and was always known as "one who got the job done". When I talked to Ron I explained how I had names and addresses from twenty-five years before, and needed help in locating at least some of these individuals. I had known before that Ron was completely capable of locating people, but when he heard the time that had lapsed between the dates of the original letters and now, he wasn't sure if he could be of help. I just kept telling him how tenacious he was, and how we all thought of him as "one who got the job done", and with my pushing and persistence he did come through. I will never forget his efforts. Without his help I would not have been able to locate some of the people who gave me the most valuable information I obtained for this book. Ron, I owe you one!!

With Ron's help I slowly began to locate people but even then it was not always easy to get them to respond. Some of the ones I did talk to and who promised to write down their thoughts regarding Jackie failed to do so. I never heard from them again. Some just plain declined to talk regarding her as they said they preferred to leave the tragedy buried in the depths of their minds. Others said to "let it lie as it brings up such hurt again" and it had all been too difficult for them to comprehend at the time, much less after all these years had passed.

Then one day I received a letter from Chris Appel, one of Jackie's close friends whom I had written to after returning from Wisconsin. She said she was in the sister company of Jackie's while in boot camp in Orlando Florida, and afterwards they were both sent to Corps School at Great Lakes where they were roommates along with Marilyn Williams. After Corps School the three of them were assigned to duty at the Naval Regional Medical Center in Yokosuka, Japan. Jackie and Marilyn were assigned ward duty and Chris was assigned to the Radiology Department, due to her civilian training as a Radiology Technologist.

Chris said in her letter how fortunate she was to have known Jackie as she was the sweetest person she had ever met, and how she always had a smile for one and showed genuine concern. She was quiet and shy, gentle and kind. She was a true, genuine person and never put on "airs" or felt she had to impress you. With her it was "what you see is what you get, and it was *all* good!" She went on to say, "In closing, I'd just like to say that Jackie quietly and gently touched your life and left a strong, everlasting impression. How lucky I was to have had her as a friend." She also suggested I contact Marilyn Williams as she and Jackie had been roommates in Japan, and Chris felt Marilyn could give me more information and more insight into Jackie's life in Japan.

CHAPTER 15

TO JACKIE,
25 YEARS LATER.....MARILYN

"I'm starting this on my daughter's twentieth birthday as I am sitting in her apartment in Cary, North Carolina, which is about four hours from my home in Asheville. I try to think back to when I was twenty and I recall that's when my life made a dramatic change. Without *truly* the kind and caring compassion of my very dearest of friends, Jackie, I would not be here in my daughter's apartment, as she sits in a classroom over at North Carolina State University. I am writing this by hand rather than using my computer as I don't want what I have to say to be on my computer. This is a very difficult journey to go back through and it will bring out some skeletons in a closet. I hope my family will understand and especially my son Ben." Thus started Marilyn Williams' recollections of her time with Jackie and their days in Japan.

"To Jackie, 25 years later.....Marilyn"

"I met Jackie in February of 1977," she began, "when we both entered the Navy at the same time. Busloads of us arrived from all over the country to spend eight weeks at boot camp in Orlando, Florida. I flew in from Denver, Colorado and Jackie came from Osceola, Wisconsin.

The Navy personnel were forming units and Jackie and I were assigned to the same barracks along with 30-40 other women. I remember she and another girl had to wind up wearing very slim men's dungarees, which looked so much nicer than the ones we had to wear! At first she was a bit out of step when we had to learn to march as a unit, but soon most everyone was in stride.

"Our unit didn't win a great many awards or flags in the various competitions pitted against other units, but we did fine for ourselves. The one thing I can tell you was that Jackie was very smart and boy, could she run! She truly enjoyed the times we had to get out and run what were called the blue line and red line. I think the blue line race was a mile and the red line race was two miles. Never-the-less, she would be one of the first people to cross the finish line. I made it eventually, doubled over and ready to puke. I get a chuckle even to this day because after I completed boot camp, I said, no more running for me. (And pretty much have stuck to that belief to this day.)

"I am trying to recall how we received information concerning the fact there would be five or six of us headed to Great Lakes, Illinois for Hospital Corps School. Maybe we just all inquired who was going into what billet or occupation and when the next training would begin. Upon graduating from boot camp, the Navy gave us two weeks of leave and then on to Corps School."

Marilyn continued in her writing to tell how when she arrived at Great Lakes it was a Saturday and things were pretty quiet. "After I signed some things in the office and received my room assignment I went to the room to drop off my things. I remember Jackie already being unpacked and she had the bed that was not the bunk bed. Soon Chris Appel arrived and also shared our room and I eventually wound up with the bottom bunk. Chris had been in another unit in boot camp that was a 'competitor' against our unit, and that unit had won many competitions against us. We weren't too sure if Chris would think she was better than us but we were wrong. Chris was just one of the gals and she and Jackie hung around at times more than Jackie and I, but Chris, at that time, also had a boyfriend named Bob.

"Just being out of Corps school and still some what in shape, plus it now being May, Jackie wanted to see if I would run with her to get some exercise. (Remember what I said earlier.) I did try to keep up with her for a few days, but that quickly came to an end. She would be half way around this park area on the base before I could even get a quarter of the way around. Forget that! We also went swimming and to movies, and I, always to this day, remember Jackie ordering a milkshake from an ice cream truck which came around every evening when she was studying. She would probably still be lean and svelte to this day, had she lived.

"Jackie of course excelled in her studies throughout Corps school. Chris was already an x-ray technician, so this was probably just a review for her. Since Corps school was just basic medical/EMT training one got sort of rushed through before being sent to work in a hospital or a naval station, or if lucky, to another training facility to further your medical training. I remember one time we all had to give each other injections and I was so nervous and didn't do a very good job, and to this day want to tell my friend and classmate, Robert, sorry you were the guinea pig for me! But Jackie was very professional in all of the lab work, exercises and exams we were responsible for doing. I am sure she finished at the top of the class when it came to the academic part of our standings.

"We did have a place to 'kick back' and relax besides going to the park or swimming, and that was going to the Enlisted Men's Club on base. We also went off base when we could find someone with a vehicle. Jackie, if she did drink anything, would just have a glass, one glass, and that was about it. Plus she most likely went back to the barracks with Chris or someone heading back while I stayed out longer and partied harder.

"I don't recall Jackie really dating anyone in particular while we were in Great Lakes, so again there were times I wasn't too sure what all she would be doing. I did start dating a classmate and friend and we found some common ground. Pat was from West Virginia, and I don't know if his southern accent was the first thing that drew me to him, or just his friendly manner and being a gentleman that made me want to be with him. So, after about a month I started to spend more time with Pat than I did with Jackie or Chris. During this time I also struck up a friendship with another friend, Dee. Dee, in most cases, was more like me than Jackie was. We both liked to go out and I felt like my ability to enjoy life was put before school. I did try to learn everything expected of us, but it wasn't first priority. I had just graduated from High School in 1976, so this was my first taste of freedom and I very much embraced it.

"Jackie did have another passion besides running and that was playing softball. She was a damn good player and athlete. I remember watching her pitch and I'm not really sure if she was actually part of a class team or it was just a bunch of sports addicts striking up a ball game. But it was fun watching the team in action.

"During the time we had been in school, Jackie's mom had been so kind in sending treats and I recall a time when Jackie was going to take a hop from Illinois to Wisconsin to see her parents. She gave me a box of cookies, brownies, etc, from her mom and said to enjoy them while she went home. I was trying not to eat so many sweets and wound up taking the box to a volleyball game and cookout and everyone fell in love with those goodies! Unfortunately, Jackie's hop didn't go out and when she returned to the barracks she asked where the box was and I showed her the now empty box. I told her I was sorry and how everyone enjoyed each piece and she just shrugged her shoulders and started unpacking.

"I believe it was around halfway through our training that we had to write down choices as to where we would like to be stationed, if possible. I don't think any of us realized just how fortunate we all were at that time, as we were a minority of service personnel that did not have to go to war or serve in a time of conflict throughout the world. That's why this is even more 'senseless' in what happened to Jackie—there will never be an answer. Anyway, since I had become good friends with Pat and I knew he was going to Virginia to further his education, I tried to request that area also. I had also requested California as I had relatives out that way. I don't recall in what order we found out we were going to Yokosuka, Japan, but it was Chris, Dee, Jackie and myself. I recalled being a bit in shock since I had not requested to go there, but we were told it was unusual this many people out of one class would be headed to the same place. Pat did his best to tell me that this would be a great adventure and that he too wanted to eventually be stationed in Yokosuka. I wasn't sure about the rest of the girls, but I do believe they were very excited about heading to Japan. It was around this time we said we were going to try and get into the same barracks and room together again."

Chapter 16
Memories of those days in Japan

"It is a pleasure to welcome you to the staff of the U.S. Naval Regional Medical Center, Yokosuka (pronounced Yo-ko-ska), Japan. We are a tenant command located at Fleet Activities, Yokosuka. The base is the largest U.S. Naval Shore Facility in the Far East and covers an area of approximately 500 acres.

"I am confident that you will find duty here to be enjoyable, both personally and professionally. You will find the medical center to be busy and your fellow staff members highly trained and energetic. There will be opportunities for you to visit places of historical interest as well as natural beauty in Japan and other parts of the Far East during your time in Yokosuka."

This was the beginning of the *Welcome Aboard* booklet sent to each of the military personnel assigned to the medical facility in Japan. The booklet was filled with brief information needed to prepare for the transfer and gave the reader an insight into what to expect when they arrived at their new home in a foreign country. It told a short history of Japan and then gave some very good reference books for follow-up reading. It also gave information on what to bring in one's household goods, such as clothing, shoes, extra military uniforms, any special needs items; enough to last the length of their tour of duty. Clothing and shoes were very difficult for Americans to buy as generally Americans are much larger than the Japanese and the local items did not fit, and special needs items would probably not be available at all. In addition to the booklet, all military and civilian personnel were required to attend an Area Orientation Briefing after arrival, which was designed to help one interact with the Japanese, and therefore enhancing tour satisfaction and job effectiveness. The United States military wanted all their personnel and family dependants to be fully informed and prepared for overseas assignments, and to not only perform well in their jobs but to be respectful of the host country's customs and tradition.

After Marilyn, Jackie, Dee and Chris arrived in Japan they were assigned rooms in the BEQ (Bachelor Enlisted Quarters), with Dee and Marilyn sharing one room and Jackie and Chris in the room next door. Chris didn't stay in the BEQ very long though, as Bob arrived in Japan shortly after Chris did and they were soon married and moved off base. Jackie then had a new roommate, Sallie Gaydos, who had been in the class behind them at corps school, and now had been assigned to Labor & Delivery. The four girls settled very quickly into their jobs and schedules. Dee went to a medical-surgical ward; Marilyn was assigned to Labor & Delivery; Jackie, being one for detail, went to ICU; and Chris who was already an x-ray technician knew what she would be doing.

Soon after their arrival they signed up for the orientations they were required to attend, and one of the first was a class to learn the local culture and how to get around by train and subway. Marilyn recalled how she and Jackie, along with the rest of the class, had been taken to Tokyo by the class instructor, and basically were dumped off with instructions to "visit a temple (bring back the ticket stub), eat lunch (bring receipt) and return to the base by 10 PM. Sharp!"

As the two young girls stood staring at the tremendous bustle of the large city, Marilyn pulled out her guide book. "The Meiji Shrine is to the right," she told Jackie. Then they both giggled at the excitement of where they were.

"Let's go," Jackie said as she headed off into the crowded street, with all her adventurism and enthusiasm.

More than once Marilyn remarked to the other girls in the barracks how focused and calm Jackie was. This day was no exception. They began walking down the street to where they could see masses of people entering the red gates. All of the people within a few inches height of each other, all with straight black hair, and bowed shoulders. Marilyn, with her long brown hair, and Jackie, tall and slender with her long, straight, light brown hair, towered over them all.

As they reached the gate, they saw to their right a car – a Datsun, it was, – parked beneath some dusty trees. A young couple and their respective parents were standing to its side, bowing and talking excitedly. A priest from the temple emerged, in a white robe, short black hat, layers of beads and silk ropes across his chest. He carried what looked like a horse-whip. He approached the car ceremoniously, slowly and solemnly, and the family quieted. He walked up to the white Datsun, obviously new by its shine and model, began to chant simple phrases and then waved the fronded whip many times at the driver's side door. He circled the car, blessing the hood, the passenger's side and the trunk, as Marilyn and Jackie held back from entering the temple. The girls looked at each other, smiled at their good luck for being in Japan rather than Osceola and Denver, and then walked through the red gated turnstile into the shrine grounds.

The walk across the grounds was hot and dusty. The grass plazas were serene, untrammeled and unused. Jackie looked around her at every detail, absorbing the exotic, unusual world of a Shinto Shrine.

There was the purification fountain near the shrine's entrance and they saw the visitors take a nearby ladle, fill it with fresh water, rinse both their hands, and then transfer the water from the ladle to their mouth. They later learned that quite a few visitors skip the mouth part of the purification ritual altogether, and they decided they would also skip that part if they ever decided to participate. The girls shed their shoes at the first step, sitting to ungainly untie their sneakers, as clusters of Japanese effortlessly slipped out of their sandals and walked on up the stairs. It was just a few steps up to the main temple room, and each step had been trod by dozens of visitors every day and the wood felt like silk beneath their feet. No wood ever felt this way before. Before leaving the shrine they saw the people in the offering hall throw a coin into the offering box, bow deeply twice, shake their clasped hands twice, bow deeply once more, and pray for a few seconds. Jackie and Marilyn dropped a few coins in the box, bowed their heads briefly and then left the shrine.

In the afternoon, they stopped at a small food shop on the Ginza, the bustling main street back to the train station, and chose their meal by pointing at the plastic samples in the window. Jackie chose beef and noodle soup.

"It tastes the closest to what my German grandmother used to make back home," she told Marilyn, who laughed at her for her consistency. "And besides, I don't have to risk biting into some octopus", she laughed, as Marilyn spit out a lump of chewy white flesh, also laughing as she hid the octopus beside her bowl.

They then headed back to the base, having bought their train tickets with a combination of sign language and pointing at their guide book, resting back into the black vinyl seats on the crowded train. Sweating youths hung over them, as their eyes closed and they murmured "success!" to each other, fingering the temple ticket stubs and the lunch receipts in their pockets. They knew they had mastered the first task and now had the confidence needed to take them through their two year tour in Japan.

Marilyn continued with her memories of Yokosuka city. In those days the city was still a blend of the old and the new, and there was much to explore that seemed exotic. They would head for the shopping streets and wander through the stores, ignoring the clothes which seemed out of style to them and also much too small, and aimed for the odd knickknacks and gifts. You could buy a scarf for carrying things – a furoshki – carefully folded, covered with cellophane and perfectly placed in a box for presenting as a gift. Vivid colors and ancient patterns covered them. Or palm-size ceramic figurines of Buddha's or gods or spirits which were also fun to look at in store after store. They planned what they would buy for Christmas gifts, which had to be mailed by October in order to be received by Christmas in the United States. Jackie always had an eye out for house wares she could send her mother and sister; unusual shaped dishes; block-printed curtains, for example.

Japan was always crowded and sometimes to avoid the crowds they would go around the corners to the back streets, through the neighborhoods, where they would pass small gates and doors to tiny houses. The ancient houses, some a mere fourteen feet wide, would be crammed in between six story concrete apartment houses. Marilyn told how one day she and Jackie peeked into an open gateway of one of those ancient houses, and the entrance to the house was only about five feet high, framed by an old forked tree trunk that was holding up the doorframe. The house had been built around a tree hundreds of years before but the tree had died, and then had been polished and preserved as the honored entrance. That day Jackie told of how on her family farm the original barn was still there, itself built around an ancient beam of a tree that her great-great-something grandfather had cut out of the woods when he had settled there.

Often Marilyn and Jackie would scurry back from one of their shopping trips, rushing through the hospital halls to get to work, still carrying the bags marked with the distinctive crest-like logo of the Japanese stores. Marilyn said she met her future husband that way, racing past a friendly guy who had just had knee surgery and was in the orthopedic ward. Everyday he teased her and asked if she had a present for him, and when she finally brought him something from town his response became the beginning of a romance leading to their thirty year marriage. After that, Marilyn and Jeff began seeing quite a bit of each other.

Marilyn and Jeff had some very rocky times during those months as they both liked to party and their work schedules were not always the same. Marilyn recalled different times when Jeff would be in the girls' rooms and had been drinking too much, but she just enjoyed being with him too much to realize this could be a problem. She felt the girls thought of him as a big brother, and none of them ever commented negatively about Jeff.

Marilyn's recollections continued. "That late winter one of the nurses with me in Labor and Delivery, who was from the Republic of the Philippines, began to suggest that Jackie and I use our standby status and 'catch a hop' with her to visit her home in the tropics. And so we did. The three of us took a week's leave and hopped down to Clark Air Force Base, near Nori's home. Jackie and I stayed with her parents in a large, wooden colonial home that was open to the tropical breezes, and yet had slum shacks built literally right against its outer walls. The mix of rich and poor was eye-opening to us. And even the rich, as Nori's family clearly were for that country, managed with lack of air conditioning, and even lack of electricity randomly throughout the day.

"But her family was warm and welcoming and hospitable, and we had an amazing time with them. After a few days we all bundled up and headed to the mountains to the resort town of Baguio, where the U.S. Air Force had an Air Station, Camp John Hay. We stayed in the BEQ's guest rooms there and enjoyed the cooler weather and mountain air, and here we truly shopped. Baguio was filled with silversmiths, hand-woven clothing shops and wooden carvings made by the native mountain people. We spent hours wandering through the open market, fingering the delicate filigree silver jewelry that is handmade there and choosing gifts for our families back home. Then moved on to the unusual clothing that was made of some kind of indigenous fiber and embellished with intricate embroidery. Everything in Baguio was intricately made, we thought perhaps because of the isolation in the mountains and the hard work it took to carve out a living in those terraced hillsides. The wood carvings were also unique, so between those, the clothes and the silver, our suitcases bulged by the time we headed back down to the coast.

"We took one last trip before we headed back to Japan. We took a cruise – a base motor boat out to an island in Subic Bay for a day of swimming and sunning. For us the day was a surprise, as the boat began to sink halfway out to the island. Holding our cameras over our heads, we laughed and celebrated as the Provost Marshal luckily came by and rescued us! With that as our finale, we headed back to the Air Force base for an endless wait for another military hop, which never arrived and resulted in our having to take a commercial flight from Manila to Tokyo. Jeff still has the wooden ashtray I bought him in Baguio, but he has worn out the shirts I purchased for him. I don't know if Phyllis still has the tie-dyed skirt and shirt Jackie bought, it was black, blue and white, I believe. Mine is dark green, tan and white. I still have mine."

CHAPTER 17

I REMEMBER HER CLUTCHING
THE ENVELOPE—

"Spring came and with it Japan's cherry blossoms. The streets of town were decorated with trees, and the town smelled like candy and the blossoms were like snow flakes all over the ground. We were glad for the warmth and the chance to get out more. Our lives grew more complex, as schedules crossed and uncrossed. Dee and I had to put foil up against our window in the bedroom so it would be dark and we could sleep during the day. We went out more with new friends, other people. Jackie did meet a very nice guy, I don't remember his name, but they dated for about three or four months. Jackie had a lot of admirers. Dee and Sallie also dated others off and on. We had just come off of working many nights and I had the opportunity to go with Jeff to one of his friend's place to spend the weekend. I really preferred staying at the barracks since I didn't like the way some of his friends blasted their stereos, but still I wanted to be with Jeff.

"I had gone back to the barracks with Jeff, to pick up some things before heading back out with him, when I heard that someone in our barracks had been attacked by a person who shouldn't have been in the barracks. I'm not sure who really told me it was Jackie who had been assaulted, but when I got to our room, she was in her room and I remember her friend Jim, who she had been seeing for a while, filling everyone in on what had happened. Jackie said she had left the door unlocked because she thought I was coming back that night. Jackie had gone to bed and around 9 PM or so, this person went into Dee's and my room first. Since neither of us were there, he went into Jackie and Sallie's room. Jackie said she thought that Jeff was just kidding around and had come in to bug her. Then she realized it wasn't Jeff and I know she tried to knock the crap out that ass. You probably know more about this than I do, but she had scratches on her and really looked shook up. But thank goodness, she seemed to be okay. She kept pretty quiet about what had happened, but I know she had put in writing her statement to the Navy Investigators. I remember her clutching the envelope so I wouldn't look in it. I just didn't know what she had written.

"That evening I told Jeff I was going to stay at the BEQ, but he didn't want me to since all of our stuff was still at his friend's place off base. I tried to get Jackie to come with us but she didn't want to go and told us to go on. I felt bad that I didn't stay and left her there alone. I can remember after my shift I pulled the foil off the window and made everything bright, and bought Jackie some flowers and told her we were so sorry this happened, and we all said we would keep the door locked from that point on.

"Later on, Jeff and I made plans to go to the American Embassy in Tokyo to get married and were trying to get a couple of witnesses to go with us. Jackie was working and everyone had a conflict and finally the only two people who could go with us were two of Jeff's good friends. We were trying to keep things very low keyed. I wore the same dress that Chris wore when she got married, which happened to be Jackie's dress! It was a pretty maroon and tan dress and I remember Jackie saying that if it brought us good luck then maybe some day she too could wear it to get married. Jeff wasn't feeling too well when we left on the train as the boys took him out for a bachelor's get together the night before, and needless to say he enjoyed them treating him to a night out. While we were heading to Tokyo, I sat there really starting to feel as if I was about to tell Jeff I didn't know if I wanted to do this. I don't know if it was just seeing him in the state he was in but we had been through so much, and why was I now thinking this way? So I never said anything to anyone and have just written this for the first time ever! We did get married at the American Embassy in Tokyo and to this day our marriage certificate that we had specially written in Kanji, hangs on the wall in our hallway at home.

"Jeff had been released by the Doctors since his knee was now okay and his date to leave Japan was moved up. He had to put in his request for where he wanted to be stationed back in the States. His family was in Asheville, North Carolina, and he requested that, plus he also put down Virginia and I know California. He still had a while before he was to rotate out but that time really went fast. I hadn't been feeling well and was a lot heavier and one day went to see one of the obstetricians for a pregnancy test. It came back negative, but I knew something was wrong. Finally, I went back to the Doctor and this time I had a positive test report. I knew Jeff was going to be mad and I was afraid to say anything to him. I guess I just sort of went on auto pilot as everything seemed to be in a fog.

"Finally one hot day I decided to tell Jeff and needless to say he wasn't very happy. In fact he didn't want to talk to me, so that's what we did, just didn't talk. The one thing that was for certain though, I didn't want to get out of the Service and I didn't want to go back to the States until my tour was over. But still, I didn't know what I was going to do. As the days drew nearer for Jeff to leave, some of his friends told me they had spoken to him about how he shouldn't leave me because

I was pregnant. I don't know what was said but I know that changed everything. I remember going in and sitting down by Jeff, we didn't say anything, but then Jeff put his arm around me, made a big sigh and said, 'Well all I can say is that it better be a boy.' Shortly after that Jeff left and was assigned to an ammunition ship, the USS Shasta (AE-33).

"All the time I was going back and forth trying to figure out what I was going to do, Jackie never judged me in whatever I was going to decide to do. I know she had her own opinion, but she didn't try to influence my decision. It wasn't her problem and she could have just washed her hands of me and said see ya later....but she didn't. In fact, she said let's go and find a place to live off base and started talking to other people who had found housing off base. If it hadn't been for Jackie, I don't know where I would have wound up or how I would have survived. Before I knew it, we had found a very nice two bedroom apartment about three miles from the base. With help from some kind friends, we got moved in and the ward even threw a baby shower for me. I really was surrounded by some very kind people at NRMC-Yokosuka. Now Jackie and I lived off base and took the bus to the base, since neither of us had a car.

"I was busy going through Lamaze and getting ready to have Ben in December and had been writing Jeff, although I didn't get many letters from him. When he did write he said he was getting settled back into living on a ship again, and that he didn't know when he could catch a hop back over to Japan. I remember I was on duty the evening of December 12th, 1978, when I started having contractions, and I remember telling the other staff at the hospital to just yell if I needed to help them out, and I went to lie down. The next morning I delivered my Ben, (I didn't know if I was going to have a boy until I actually had him), and I kept saying thanks to God. That afternoon Jackie came into my room and she picked up Ben and she had such a big and bright smile, and I knew she had already fallen in love with Benny right at that moment. I had also sent a message to Jeff via the American Red Cross, and had called my parents and I remember my dad was getting ready to go to work and when I said, 'Hi, Grandpa', my mom said dad cried. Jackie was so helpful to me in bringing me items from home that I had forgotten and also taking my stuff back to the apartment, and when I returned home she had decorated the apartment with a little Christmas tree we had used in the barracks the year before. I remember getting letters from Jeff's mom and how she wanted to make sure I was taking care of her grandson, but I still had not heard very much from Jeff. But I was happy with having Ben and Jackie near me.

"I only took a month maternity leave as the personnel office at the hospital had been working to get me switched over to the Pediatric Clinic and I wanted that position before someone else took it. One day Sallie told me to follow her down to the main hallway and there was Jeff with his back to me. Everyone gave us a few minutes to ourselves, then one of the nurses let us use her car and we bought groceries and Jeff met Ben when we picked him up from the babysitter's. Jeff bought a lot of things at the commissary and I told him we didn't have much money and we needed to be cautious, but we had enough to last while he was on leave. Since I had just started back to work, I couldn't take any time off, all I could do was work out a long weekend. Jackie was the proud aunt telling Jeff all of the stories we already had on Ben.

"The first evening that Jeff was at our apartment, he sat and held Ben for a long time, and then said how happy he was to be a dad and have a beautiful son that he would play ball with, and teach to ride a bike, and do all the things that a dad and son would do. So for that moment, things seemed to be all perfect in the world. But in just a few days, such a short time, Jeff had to head back to his ship, but I think he was glad we had the opportunity to be together as it would be another year before we would see each other again. From February 1979 until December 1979.

"One day I asked Jackie if she would be Ben's Godmother and she said she would be truly happy to do so. Living so far away from family had really been hard on all of us. I had all my troubles, which in retrospect I know I was fully responsible for, but at that young age I just felt the world was against me at times. But knowing Jackie would be the one responsible for my Ben, if something ever happened, at least set my mind at ease on that matter. And also, just to show what wonderful people Mr. and Mrs. Wurst are, after Jackie was killed they assumed her responsibilities as Ben's Godparents. Jackie certainly had a rough time also, and the rest of us just hoped we had been some comfort to her in her time of need. Jackie never talked about being attacked after the incident happened, except once to swear she would never let something like that ever happen to her again. She said she would fight to the end if someone ever tried that again. But good things do happen and within just a couple of months she had met Carl, and things were pretty nice for her then."

Marilyn put down her pen, folded her hand-written sheets of paper, and included some photos she had taken during their time together in Japan, then placed it all in a thick manila envelope and mailed it off to me. Her life, her memories, good and bad, but mostly what a wonderful friend Jackie had been to her in the darkest part of her life.

Jackie in Kyoto, Japan at Three Sisters Inn, May 1979

Jackie in front of U.S. Navy Fleet Activities, Yokosuka, Japan

Jackie and Marilyn Williams in Japan

Tony Carotenuto and Dee Murphy holding Ben at his baptism in Japan, 1978

Jackie and Ben Williams in Japan

CHAPTER 18

SHE MADE A POSITIVE IMPACT ON ME, ON HOW PRECIOUS LIFE IS AND HOW IMPORTANT IT IS TO LOVE SOMEONE.

Carl. Carl Tresnak. There was that name again. The one Phyllis so quietly had suggested I try to contact, and now Marilyn had also mentioned him. The address I had for Carl was once again more than twenty-five years old, and it was not even his but was his father's---just a contact address. With the bad luck I was having with all the other addresses I had, I didn't have much hope with this one. Yet, my hunch told me this person probably could be a big help, if I could only locate him. Again, I mailed a letter to the known address and again it came back, like many others I had written. I checked the local phone book and there was a listing for a Tresnak, but after making repeated calls to the number and never receiving return calls, I finally gave up on that number. The last name was so unusual, not a Smith or Jones or Johnson, I hoped if Carl Tresnak was in California I could find him. But if he had stayed in the Navy all these years would he still be here? Or would he have perhaps retired in another state, one where he might have been reassigned? But California was his home state and the address I had was his father's. Chances were he was here, but where?

My best source for helping me was my good friend Ron Janson and again I called him. Together we discussed where Carl possibly could be and came to a conclusion to try the San Diego area. Most of the other Navy bases in California had been closed by the government, and if Carl had stayed in the Navy he could possibly be one of the many retirees now living in the San Diego area. With that unusual last name there were not too many listings fortunately, so Ron "spun his little Ouiji Board" as I always tease him of doing, and came up with a number for me to call. I made my call and just received a voice mail, but left a message giving my name and explaining I was a former NIS Special Agent, and was calling regarding the Jackie Wurst murder case, and if this was the right person would he please return my call.

It seemed as though I had just made the call when my phone rang and the voice said, "Yes," he was the right Carl Tresnak. The shock to him hearing from someone regarding Jackie Wurst was very evident in his voice, and more than once I could hear his voice crack with sorrow and grief as we talked about those days so long ago. His questions were the same as I had from Jackie's family. Why was I involved at this late date? What was my motive? What did I hope to accomplish?

Carl, as I found out in this first conversation, had been dating Jackie before she left Japan and the two of them were very much in love. The separation, after she had been reassigned to Lemoore, was extremely difficult and being two young military persons they didn't have the money to travel from Japan to the United States to see each other. They counted on letters and an occasional phone call to keep in touch. Carl began saving his money for a trip home to see Jackie and did manage to do so after about six months. That was the last time he saw her. When she was killed he was not allowed to return for the funeral. He was not a family member, not a husband and not a fiancé, so the Navy would not fund his trip home, and he personally did not have the funds to pay for the trip. He said he had always planned on going to the grave site to say his goodbye's and still hoped to do so.

While talking with Carl I told him of the visit I had with the Wurst family in Wisconsin and how I had copies of various letters and photos. One particular photo which I liked and Don, Jackie's father, had said was his favorite also, had been taken in Yosemite with those famous mountains as a background. I commented that it looked like Jackie was in heaven with that surreal background. I e-mailed the photo to Carl as we were talking so he could see what I was referring to and his quick gasp was, "I took that photo, and she is in heaven."

Carl said he had stayed in the military for over thirty-two years and had attained the rank of Commander, in the Medical Service Corp, (MSC) when he finally retired. At the time when they were in Japan, he had been a Hospital Corpsman, HM2, where he also was assigned to the Hospital in Yokosuka and worked in the Lab. After leaving Japan he was reassigned to the Naval School Health Sciences, San Diego, where he was an instructor and made the rate of HM1. His next assignment was in Washington, DC, where he worked for the Attending Physician for the U.S. Congress. While there he was recognized for his outstanding ability and was selected to be commissioned, and was sent to Officers' Candidate School in Rhode Island. He was commissioned in August 1987, made the rank of Commander in July 2003, and retired in March 2005. Having just recently retired from the Navy, his current civilian position is the Deputy Chief of Staff for Human Resources Navy Medicine West, San Diego. He also explained the phone number I had previously tried calling was his father's, however his father had passed away and his stepmother just failed to pass on the phone messages to him. Shortly after our conversation ended I received the following e-mail from Carl.

"Tom,

"Needless to say, our phone conversation today floods back many memories. As you can probably tell, I've never really gotten over what happened to Jackie, it is something that I can't really wrap my mind around. To say she didn't deserve what happened in her life is an understatement. I like to remember the way she was, not the horrible way she died.

"She was genuine, she was kind, she was beautiful. It sounds so cliché but the old saying that she was as beautiful on the inside as she was on the outside rings true. Actually more so. She was a sailor and a Hospital Corpsman that had pride in her work, pride in her service and even though she was quiet she was confident. She never said 'my God', it was 'my gosh', actually I never heard her swear at all. She was trusting even though her trust had been shaken. Her faith and her family were very important to her, but she didn't judge anyone (including me) who didn't believe what she did. She was easily embarrassed, she would turn red if she got a little too much attention, she was surprised when chosen as the best female athlete on the base and very humble, saying other girls deserved it more. She was fun and enjoyed exploring new things and going places. I've always said that there are few people that make this world a better place and Jackie was one of them.

"I apologize for getting emotional, but the pain that cuts through right to your heart really never goes away. As I said, I'm a better person for knowing her that short time over twenty-five years ago. She made a positive impact on me, on how precious life is and how important it is to love someone. I'll try to put on paper some memories I have of Jackie as a tribute to her is never too late, even twenty-five years later.

Carl"

Carl and I had, and continue to have to this day, many phone conversations and e-mails in which Carl has poured out his story to me in great detail. Much of what he said was private and I do respect his privacy and promised not to print everything he wrote. His memories are so vivid and he has retained everything connected to Jackie with the exception of some personal letters that he had turned over to NIS at the time of her death. NIS had requested them to see if there was perhaps some information included which might help to identify her killer. Carl, under the Freedom of Information Act, (FOIA) has requested the letters be returned to him; however, as of this date NIS had not returned those letters which is a sore point with Carl, and one which I had to deal with in my talking with him. He still has the Fuji Stick which Jackie gave him after she had climbed Mt. Fuji in Japan. He has all the photos of the two of them they had taken while together. When I commented on how surprised I was that he still had all these items after so long he wrote back, "Why did I keep them?? How could I throw it away!! The state of shock has lasted twenty-five years."

This has been a difficult experience for Carl to return to, however as he has said many times, the tragedy has always been right up front in his mind and heart and one he can not, nor will not, ever forget. Both Carl and I do feel the first attack on Jackie, and her determination to never let it happen again, was the reason she fought so hard to her death. After Jackie's death Carl took up Karate and earned his Black Belt, and then taught classes to young women on how to defend themselves against an attacker in a way that will save their lives.

Carl did move on with his life as he had a bright future ahead of him. From a young enlisted sailor, who felt there were too many obstacles to overcome to continue with the girl of his dreams, he rose to a high ranking officer and then retired into a prestigious civilian job. He obviously is a brilliant, hard working individual to have obtained what he has. I still have not had the opportunity to meet Carl in person but have been able to form a true friendship over the phone and the Internet. He is a sensitive, articulate, and caring person and I do respect him and admire him.

As promised in that first phone call, a few days later I received a long e-mail from Carl which I am including.

"Tom,

"Wanted to share a few things that I've been thinking about, some observations, some memories and general information that may make your book more accurate

"Jackie was always alert. She looked you in the face. She walked fast. She had a purpose to her actions. She stood ram-rod straight. She sat straight. She never slouched. She had the habit of being uncomfortable about her arms, such as how to place them and where to put her hands, so when she talked she often crossed them behind the small of her back. I never saw her put her hands in her pocket unless she was getting something out. Her hair was always perfectly styled and always parted on the left side. Her hair was fluffy soft and always smelled of Breck shampoo, I'm not sure they still make it. She wore perfume but only a trace, you had to be close to smell it. I never saw her with makeup on, maybe a little lipstick but no eye makeup that I could see. Her teeth were white but not perfectly straight, she had kind of a little slightly bent upper left tooth that was a little crooked. Jackie felt kind of self conscious about that tooth, but you can't even see it in pictures.

"She was strong and tough, had great upper body strength for a woman and could actually arm wrestle very well, even against men. Her waist was thin and she had slender hips. She didn't wear high heels that I ever saw, and always had flat shoes even in a dress. In uniform she was always immaculate, always wore a fresh sharply pressed set of whites. She was respectful, polite, courteous and friendly. Her work interactions were always friendly, but never personal in the sense that she talked about herself or shared her feelings. People knew her, but didn't know about her, if that makes sense. She was a great listener, but not much of a talker. She would listen intently, and provide excellent feedback or advice, she had an opinion on things, but would only offer it if asked. She was not judgmental, and seemed accepting of just about everyone. She didn't talk behind a person's back and wouldn't spread gossip. She was religious, but her views were private, she didn't share them. She softly said grace before she ate, very quiet and personal.

"She liked to hold hands, she liked to be held, she was a great kisser but all in private most of the time. We passed a point in our relationship that the public show of affection was OK, not sure what exactly prompted it but the trust was just there at that point. Trust and honesty were important to her, she was cautious before she totally trusted someone. She was not paranoid or fearful, but she was cautious.

"Music. I've thought a lot about the type of music she liked and my memory has faded on that specific subject. I couldn't tell you what her favorite group or song was, but she always enjoyed the music I played. We did go to see the group Heart in concert (I have pictures of the stage as well as Jackie from that concert) and I remember listening to music with her in my room. I still have a lot of my vinyl albums from those days and I know we listened to the groups Chicago, the Commodores (Lionel Ritchie's group), the Beatles, Creedence Clearwater Revival, Dire Straights, the Eagles, Elton John, Gordon Lightfoot, Led Zeppelin, Neil Young, Crosby, Stills and Nash, Cat Stevens, Santana and Fleetwood Mac. I do remember writing the words of a song to her called *Color My World* by Chicago. It just seemed to fit the way I felt about her.

"I hope this helps. Good talking to you tonight as always.

Carl"

CHAPTER 19

I ASKED AGAIN, "KILLED, WHAT DO YOU MEAN KILLED??"

In October 2005, I had made that journey to the Wurst farm in Wisconsin and had made my relationship with the Wurst family even closer. One night after my return, I was telling Carl how wonderful Phyllis and Don are and what a wonderful experience it was to visit with them, and to hear their story of Jackie. I knew Carl had written a letter to them shortly after Jackie's death as Phyllis had shown it to me. Jackie had Carl buy a Japanese tea set for her sister, Charlene, and he was originally planning to bring it in his household goods when he rotated back to the United States. After Jackie's death he mailed the set to Phyllis for Charlene and sent along an accompanying letter. It was a very emotional letter, one which tried to express his grief and give his condolences to the family. It was obviously written by a young man who had never been in the position of writing such a letter before, and though well written, did not fully convey his sorrow or his closeness to Jackie. When I was talking with him, he remarked how he thought perhaps he could now write to Phyllis and Don, and inform them of his true feelings for their daughter, and at the same time let them know she would never be forgotten.

Jackie Wurst in Yosemite in March 1980

On November 30, 2005, Carl sent the following letter to Phyllis and Don, and with their permission and also that of Carl, I include it with only minor parts extracted. Some parts are too personal and as I promised Carl, I do respect his privacy.

"Dear Phyllis,

"Thank you again for being so gracious on the phone. I can't imagine how painful some memories must be for you and your family, as these memories have literally broken my heart again, much like those dark days in 1980. My tears seem strange to me as I distinctly remember how I couldn't cry then, as much as I wanted too. I remember wandering aimlessly around the base in Yokosuka, Japan – literally day and night trying to reconcile the tragedy of losing Jackie. It certainly doesn't make any more sense now than it did then, but the tears come more easily now and seem to help somehow. I have only now been able to recognize that it was easier to just suppress those feelings as confronting them was too much to bear.

"Many events in my life have been directly or indirectly influenced by her life and untimely death, but the opportunity to positively reflect on her life, even after all these years, seems like a good thing to do. I will be helping Tom Brannon with his book in any way I can, a tribute to Jackie can never come too late. My only fear about this book is Jackie will be remembered only as a victim, not as a wonderful person she really was.

"I would like to share a few things with you and Don as any remembrance of Jackie should include the truth. Please excuse me for taking liberty in sharing Jackie's relationship with me, I can't ask her permission to share but I'm thinking she wouldn't mind. (I'm thinking she would flash that certain sweet smile we still see in her pictures just to confirm that it was OK.)

"I have to admit that I'm still a little puzzled to this day that she showed me the least bit of interest. You have to understand that there was literally a line of guys that yearned, for lack of a better word, to date her. It wasn't that Jackie wasn't friendly or unapproachable or aloof, she just was sure of what she wanted to do with her time and what relationships she was willing to 'invest' in. She was beautiful in such a natural way, I don't remember her wearing makeup to speak of, and she really didn't need it. She was professional in her job, took her work very seriously and was mature about her responsibilities.

"She had a passion for sports and excelled. I often kidded her that she *didn't* throw like a girl! The irony is that I got to know her because she played on the base women's softball team and I played on the men's team. She certainly wasn't typical of a serious softball player; she was thin and feminine and smiled often on the field. She looked kind of frail until you saw her in action, lightning fast and very competitive, there was no doubt she played to win. (But very gracious, just like her Mom; in defeat, congratulating the other team on their victory.) She used to tell me that she was a tom-boy while growing up and I always said 'there is certainly no boy in you', but I was a little biased of course.

"After one such game I made an effort to meet this beautiful girl, not really knowing much about her. (Seems we never really crossed paths at the hospital because I was a lab technician and worked mainly days and she worked in the ICU at the other end of the hospital, and worked evenings and nights.) On the bus ride back to the base after the game, I sat next to her and proceeded to jabber on for about an hour-and-a-half as we rode through Tokyo. Jackie was a good listener and I was a good talker so the conversation was decidedly one way. I was thinking that night, Carl you are truly an idiot, not letting Jackie get a word in edgewise. I was sure at that point the odds of her actually going out with me were slim, and that she just was talking to me to be polite.

"The next day at work I asked around to some of my friends if they knew anything about Jackie, specifically did she have a boyfriend? After all, since I hadn't really heard her say much I didn't even know if she was available to date. The consensus was that she was a great girl that didn't seem to date much, lived off base, and kind of kept to herself. There were also murmurs of how she had been 'attacked' when she first got to Japan and how this made her kind of 'distant'. I remember clearly thinking who could do such a thing to such a sweet girl?

"I decided I needed to formulate a plan where I saw her regularly, despite our schedules, which essentially meant that I would accidentally (on purpose) run into her. I found out what her schedule was and just happened to be in the hospital when she was around. (I lived in the barracks next door, so popping over to the hospital was easy.) Much to my amazement this pitiful strategy seemed to work and she actually gave me the time of day! We talked and talked; I even listened these times, and found we had much in common. Jackie had a good sense of humor and didn't even mind when I kidded about her mid-west accent (which really wasn't that pronounced) or that I could strike her out if I wanted to in softball. (Fortunately she never took me up on that challenge as she might have proved me wrong.)

"Anyway, we seemed to hit it off, and I found myself completely taken by her. One night she got off at 11 PM and I came over to see her before she went home. We talked and laughed in the hospital hallway for almost an hour until I realized she still had to catch the train home off base and I shouldn't keep her any longer. In my mind, and my heart of course, I wanted to kiss her really badly but I was hesitant as we really hadn't even dated yet. I asked her if we could do something together that weekend and she kind of laughed and said 'what took you so long to ask me?' I must have looked so shocked that she would go out with me that she said 'I'll see you tomorrow and she gave me a hug!' That night, after I floated back to the barracks, I couldn't resist the urge to pump my fist in the air and yell 'She actually likes me!!'

"I can't actually remember where we went that weekend, I think it was just out to dinner, but I do remember she was dressed in something other than her Navy or softball uniform. I still remember, actually quite vividly, how great her hair smelled and how soft it was. She was so unassuming that I really don't think she knew the impact she had on guys and of course on me. I remember that night as I walked her to the train that I held her hand, and she actually seemed pleased that I wanted to. When we got to the station I started to tell her what a great time I had and I noticed she was looking at me funny, with a slight smile on her face. As if to say, of course 'we' had a great time, like I was crazy to have to tell her. I kissed her then, just once, and just for a few seconds. It was sweet and pure and expressed more than we could say in words. I knew I could love her then, after one kiss, I also hoped that she could love me too.

"Our relationship took off like fireworks after that. I spent as much time as I could with her as the sobering fact was that she would be leaving Japan way too soon. She had gotten stationed in Japan about a year before I got there so she would be leaving a little less than halfway through my two year tour. I am sad to say that many, many of the times we had together are very fuzzy memories. I do remember many of the fun times we had, but the time-line of our days together seems lost after all these years. If you don't mind I'd like to share a few in no particular order.

"**Japan Jam**; funny name for a rock concert. Jackie and I had much the same taste in music although she went more for the soft rock and I liked the guitars. (I sent a series of pictures from that day, the one where Jackie has on the yellow shirt is my favorite.) I remember that day well because we had so much fun, and enjoyed each other's company so much that by the end of the day was when I really thought I had fallen in love. I'm really not sure how long we had been dating when we went to the concert that day, but it was certainly a turning point on a blossoming relationship. You can even see by the pictures that she starts the day looking kind of shy and reserved and later she looks radiant. That was the first time she let me kiss her in front of our friends, I'm pretty sure I had a picture of that kiss but I can't find it anymore. (I'd love to find that yellow shirt too, but I think it's lost after all these years.) Falling in love brings so many emotions, and by this time Jackie and I started thinking about the future and our pending separation. Jackie, as you know, was a very practical woman and she asked in a very matter of fact way if we should be getting 'serious' at this point. That was my turn to laugh and I remember saying 'how can we not?'

Jackie at "Japan Jam" in 1979

"Trip to Monkey Island; there is a small island in the middle of Tokyo Bay called Monkey Island. Jackie and I decided to take a boat over and enjoy the sun and a picnic. We walked and explored for a couple of hours, looking at the WWII lookout sites and hiking through the underbrush. I took a lot of pictures that day because it was a good reason to look at Jackie, posing her here and there. She was amazed I loved looking at her so much, but my heart wouldn't let me look away. It was hot that day and I was surprised to find out she had her bathing suit on under her clothes!! She sunbathed and we had a picnic lunch and we were so comfortable together. I felt she trusted me so much that day; she just opened up and was herself. I felt pretty lucky that she was comfortable enough with me to sunbath, but of course there wasn't anyone else around that might see her! We had a picnic and enjoyed each others company; it was one of those days that I can honestly say was one of the best of my life. The kind of day that turns the corner on the sweet beginning of getting to know someone, to understand their feelings and fears and hopes for the future. She was always positive, never really pessimistic about life or problems. Jackie got a little bit of sunburn and I remember kidding her about being a pale Wisconsin girl.

"**Shopping and eating in Tokyo**; we went out to shop (which I dislike intensely to this day but it was the company that counted) and we had a nice meal in downtown Tokyo. The time kind of flew by and before we knew it we were late getting to the last train. This became a little awkward as we wondered what the heck we would do now, places were closing and we didn't have enough money to take a cab back. Let me say at this point that I always respected Jackie's morals, values and religious beliefs. She was certainly not a girl to stay in a hotel with me even though we were in love by this time. I don't say that to protect her memory, but I say that because it was true. She was comfortable about what was right and proper and appropriate. She was a 'good girl' and I respected that about her.

Jackie in Japan 1979

"We decided to walk to the Sanno Hotel, a U.S. military run hotel in Tokyo, to see if there was anything still open. No luck, but we got a great idea! We snuck out to the pool area that was really closed and kind of dark. We pulled two chaise lounges together and decided to sleep there that night. I remember the sky was clear and the stars were sparkling although it was a little chilly. (I was mainly chilly actually because I'm a California boy!!) We never really slept much, we held hands and talked and had a few of those quiet moments that were really not awkward at all, as we were very comfortable together. That kind of time is the kind that people write songs about, the kind that when you are eighty years old you still remember. The smells and the sounds and the taste of that last kiss before we left. We took the first train back at dawn, closer than ever and joined in our hearts.

"Tournament softball game; during the summer when we went out, I mentioned before that we both played on the base softball teams. This particular tournament required that we bus out to another base, an Air Force base actually. We played a few games in the morning and had a few in the afternoon if you were still winning. The problem was that the girl's team was playing quite a distance from the men's team and I didn't get to see Jackie's games. I thought after lunch I would get to see her, and our game didn't start for an hour-and-a-half so I jogged across the base to the other field to watch her game. They were winning of course but Jackie said I made her nervous watching her play.

"Time went by and all of a sudden I remembered I needed to get back for my game! I told Jackie 'good luck' and took off running and arrived just ten minutes before game time. The coach was so mad at me that he didn't let me play that game and we eventually lost. (Not because I didn't play, we just got beat.) Meanwhile on the other side of the base the girls won their tournament and everyone was excited. On the ride back to the base Jackie asked how we did and I told her we lost and I didn't get to play because I was late for warm-ups. The amazing thing about Jackie was right then it was not important to celebrate her victory, but more important to console me about our loss and not getting to play. She was amazing in the depth of her good heart, she wanted to help, she wanted to make a difference in cheering someone up and she loved me too. The amazing depth of Jackie's compassion and loving nature was never so evident as then.

"Jackie wasn't the typical 'Navy' girl. She didn't drink (not that I remember) or smoke and I never heard her cuss. (Except for once and I'll talk about that later.) She was polite and well mannered, respectful to everyone and much more intelligent than she let on. By the way, when a person enters the military they are tested to measure intelligence, aptitude, mechanical ability, etc. Jackie scored in the 99th percentile in intelligence, a perfect score is 70 and she had a 68. We joked about this as I scored a 69 and she was the only person I ever knew that scored as high as me. She used to say, when I was being smart-alecky, that I wasted that one point I had on her.

"She was also careful about letting her feelings out. I knew she trusted me but as much as we talked I always thought she was holding back. After much coaxing and hugging and reassurance, she did share her feelings about the 'attack' that happened when she got to Japan. Turns out she was racked with guilt that she didn't fight back enough, believe it or not. She felt if she had resisted more maybe she could have fought him off. I remember distinctly telling her none of us can predict how we would react in the same situation, when we are surprised and terrified and in shock. It was certainly not her fault, and she shouldn't feel guilty about it. I told her if she had resisted more, he might have hurt her more. She cried and called the guy a name in anger and I held her and told her she would be alright now and she was precious and wonderful, and this did not reflect on her but on the -------that did it. She looked at me with tears in her eyes but with a clear resolve and said, 'I would never let that happen to me again'. We never talked about it again.

"Jackie's transfer date seemed to arrive in an instant. We really hadn't been together that long, maybe three months total. I'm ashamed to say I've forgotten how much time it really was, but it really flew by. We were in love and happy and seeing a future together and started many beautiful memories and she was leaving! This was in August 1979, and I was looking at another fifteen months in Japan without her. She couldn't even extend in Japan at that point because her orders were written, and they certainly wouldn't let me leave early to be with my girlfriend. (If you get married, you will be transferred together but we both knew that our relationship was too new to even consider that, after all, she was a practical woman and knew that we shouldn't do anything we would regret no matter how she felt about me.)

"When Jackie left we talked about how we would keep in touch, she said she would write me every day, and we could occasionally talk on the phone. In 1979 there were of course no cell phones and I lived in the barracks so I didn't even have a residential phone. We could call back to the States on the military phone, but the system was for 'official business' and the operator would cut you off if it sounded too personal. The system only worked base to base so I couldn't call her at home so Jackie would write me and say she would be at a certain number in the hospital at a certain time and on a certain day. About 50 percent of the time the operator would cut us off after the first few minutes so each call was usually just a tease. I called using the pay phone a number of times but at almost fifty cents a minute in those days a young second-class really couldn't afford too many calls.

"Jackie kept her word and wrote me almost every day. I looked forward to mail call every day and was disappointed when I didn't get a letter. (Jackie rarely disappointed me though.) The very sad thing is the Navy NIS personnel took all my letters from Jackie to 'assist' in their investigation after she was killed. I tried to tell them they were love letters from a girlfriend to a boyfriend and having someone else read her letters seemed like such a violation of her privacy. (The letters never said anything about anyone bothering her or threatening her.) I was angry that they forced me to give them up and I never got them back. (I assume they were destroyed at some point because even though I had written several times to attempt to get them back all they said was they were lost.)

"After the holidays, I told Jackie that I really needed to come back to the States and visit her. The letters and few phone calls a month were not enough, I missed her greatly. I started planning to visit her and put in for leave and started saving my money for plane tickets. (I have forgotten the exact date I came back but I think it was some time in May or June.) The time dragged on and by spring softball started again and we both had a distraction from the loneliness of missing each other. The day I went to the airport to come back to the States for the visit was truly gut wrenching. I really missed Jackie tremendously, but I started thinking we actually had been separated almost twice as long as we had been together. What if things had changed? What if we didn't feel the same about each other now? What if she moved on in her life? Because being in the States is a lot different than being stationed overseas. Overseas, the military people become very close because we all shared that 'away from home' feeling. Overseas, people do a lot of things together because it's hard to make friends with people off base that don't speak English.

"I flew home to San Francisco and Jackie was at the airport to meet me. She was so beautiful and soft and her hair smelled just like I remembered and I just held her for a long time. I was surprised she appeared kind of shy around me and it was just kind of uncomfortable in some ways, but I chalked that up to six months of separation. We had planned a trip that would include visiting my Dad in the San Francisco bay area and driving up to my sister's house in eastern California. We also wanted to spend some time together so we decided to go to Yosemite National Park and drive over to the coast and see Santa Barbara and Monterey.

"I only had ten days of leave so our plans included a lot of driving. We kept our plans and held hands and talked and hugged and got to know each other again, but it was clear the expectation of this reunion was very high, maybe impossibly high. A lot had happened in those six months apart. I could see the intense feeling generated by those wonderful days in Japan seemed to be a long time ago, and had faded more than we wanted. We had missed out on the part of the relationship where you become best friends with the woman you love. We never had the routine days, the ones where you just read or watch TV together. We never thought much about practical things or where we would work or if we would go to school. I know Jackie wanted to be a nurse like Charlene, but she never said where she would go to school.

"As we traveled around those days, we talked about the future and what we wanted from life. She wanted out of the Navy by then and I had committed to another four years by reenlisting. We talked about California (she didn't like it that much, but Lemoore is really pretty desolate), and Wisconsin and religion and our feelings about life's issues. In Japan it was about us and it was intense and loving and a celebration of that specific time and moment. Now it seemed we had a little dose of reality about what we could or should have together, and if we could work out continuing our relationship with more than six months of separation in front of us.

"I really started feeling sad and confused and uncertain the more we talked because the time was flying by, and before we knew I would be heading back to Japan. I told her how I was feeling and she started to cry and asked me if I still loved her? I wish I could articulate how I felt at that very point. My heart shouted that 'of course I love you', but I had doubts that our whirlwind romance was genuine committed love. I told Jackie it was not about love but about whether it was right we commit after so little time together. Let me say at this point I had always thought Jackie deserved more than me, I always kind of thought she was basically too good for me. I'm certainly not a bad person; don't get me wrong, I don't mean that. It was just that she had a very idealistic way about her, she had very high standards and morals and expectations. She 'never' judged me or anyone else, don't get me wrong, but I felt guilty when I cussed around her. She was always kind of naïve about some things, even though she was a mature person. I'm sorry to be so blunt, but I said I would tell you the truth.

"This is the part that hurts so much and I have felt guilty about it for over twenty-five years now. I told Jackie then I thought we should cool our relationship as I was having second thoughts about what the future held for us. When the words came out of my mouth I thought it was the right thing to do, but I've never thought that since. She was sweet and strong and still took me to the airport the next day. I held her and kissed her goodbye and knew when our lips met I was making a mistake. Seeing her for the last time without that special smile and with tears coming down her cheeks, is something I would give anything to change now. Our last minutes together were sad, and I regret being stupid and self-centered and short-sighted. The way things turned out encouraged me to bury this guilt as far and as deep as I could because that part was too hard to bear.

"Jackie continued to write me after I got back to Japan but I only talked to her on the phone two or three times after that. The time kind of went by and I threw myself into softball and continued on. The occasional letter from Jackie would let me know how she was doing and things she had done, but we were reduced to friends at that point and it was sad. She always signed her letters, 'Love, Jackie' and I did the same back, but it wasn't the same. I actually suggested to her during that time for her to challenge the LVN exam as I had done that myself. She talked a lot about going to nursing school and was making plans and I encouraged her as much as I could.

"During this time, I of course had second, and third, and fourth….thoughts about ending the relationship with Jackie. I wasn't sure what to do so I decided to write her and suggest we meet for the holidays and talk. I wanted to tell her that I still loved her and I had just gotten scared and I made a mistake. I sent that letter near the end of September 1980, and I'm not sure she ever got it. I still wonder to this day.

"I was at work in the lab in Japan when my boss called me in and said Jackie had been 'killed'. I remember saying, 'killed, what do you mean she was killed??' The impact of the news was devastating and numbing. I had never really understood a person being in shock before that moment. The world kind of rolled up and became a narrow tube and there were distant voices on the other end. I asked again, 'killed, what do you mean killed??' He looked at me sadly and said she had been murdered. No, No, NO, NO, NO!!!! Not Jackie, it must be a mistake, this couldn't happen to such a kind sweet person!!!!

"I walked away and just headed down the street. Couldn't cry, couldn't think, couldn't understand. I still don't understand, I don't think I ever will.

"The days in Japan after that are a blur. The only way I could get through the day was work hard and go for a long run after work. I ran until I dropped a few times. I remember running during a typhoon that was rolling through the area. I thought if I got hit by a tree it may be okay. There was no reconciling, no developing an understanding, no ability to cope, just wondering why over and over. Just run and concentrate on putting one foot in front of the other. I still run to this day at least three times a week.

"Robert Kennedy once said after the assassination of President Kennedy that 'we should not elevate him in death, more than he was in life'. Jackie wasn't perfect; she had her faults just like the rest of us. But in her case there was no need to elevate her, she was special and better than most of us. That is the simple truth. You can certainly be proud of the wonderful daughter, woman, human being that was and still is alive in many, many hearts. I'm sure she is an image of a wonderful family that raised and endowed her with such great principles and standards and kindness. She made a difference to almost everyone who had contact with her, she brought a smile to so many faces, and she showed us how we could all be better people. We all could only hope to have such a legacy.

I'm personally better for having known her, and exceptionally fortunate to have been loved by her. I'll miss her always.

"A lot has happened to me over the past twenty-five years, but I won't bore you with my life. I'm exceptionally lucky in many ways and I'm thankful for the opportunities and successes I've had. I'm letting my wife Deanna read this letter as she has good enough judgment to let me know if it's the right thing to do. To think that I loved and was loved by two exceptional, wonderful loving women, first Jackie and now Deanna, in one lifetime makes me not only lucky but thankful indeed.

Warmest Regards,
Carl

"P.S. Phyllis, you certainly can share this letter if you want. I will respect Jackie's privacy and ask your permission to share this with Tom Brannon for his book. If it is too personal I will understand. Again, give my best to Charlene.

"P.S.S. Garth Brooks wrote a song called *The Dance*; it always made me think of Jackie and me."

Later, I received an e-mail from Carl regarding this letter and he again reiterated how he was racked with guilt through the years for his youthful actions, and how he has always wondered if she ever received the last letter he sent her. He also emphasized again to me, "Tom – my only hope is that she is not remembered as a victim, but as the loving, caring, wonderful person she was. It's not about how she died but how she lived. I trust you to make sure everyone understands that my friend and I will help you. Carl"

CHAPTER 20

A VERY GOOD FRIEND WHO ACTUALLY HELPS YOU THROUGH WHEN YOU ARE ALL ALONE.

In June 2006, my wife and I made a trip to Ashville, North Carolina to finally meet Marilyn Williams, Jackie's close friend. I had talked with her on the phone and received a number of e-mails from her but I was eager to talk face to face with her regarding Jackie. In my investigative years I always felt that a one-on-one interview was more productive as one then could get a true picture of the other person's feelings and emotions.

We arrived in Ashville and called Marilyn to let her know we were in town and she said she and Jeff were waiting for us and dinner was ready. They live only a few minutes out of town, up a country road, and into a hilly area. We almost missed the driveway but then realized the woman waving at us was Marilyn, letting us know where to turn in. The driveway was bordered on each side with Azaleas and Rhododendrons in full bloom. After a short distance we went over a small bridge with a creek running below, and then on up to the house. It is a beautiful setting, with a very large Oak tree in the center of the front lawn. A tree so large that its canopy covers the complete front. The house backs up against a hill covered in lush green plants and trees and has a small patio in the rear where we discovered the table set and dinner waiting for us to enjoy. Jeff was the cook and what a great cook he is!

Marilyn and Jeff definitely know how to show their southern hospitality and we instantly felt as though we had known them both for many years. Jeff has a wonderful sense of humor and with our common Navy background I found I got along very well with him. Marilyn was busy trying to make everything perfect for our outdoor dinner, like most wives do. We no sooner started to eat when a sudden, summer rain shower passed over. We could hear the rain hitting the trees above us but the foliage was so dense it took some time before we could actually feel the rain. Suddenly we knew we had to move, and everyone started grabbing food and dishes and quickly moved everything inside to the dining room. We just laughed and said, "so much for outdoor dining!"

We began our conversations with the beauty of the area and then Jeff told us his stories of the bears in the hills out back where we had first started our dinner party. Seems they wander thru the yard quite often, and now that we were safe inside, we periodically looked out to see if there were any visiting that evening. He also reminded us that not too far away in a thick, densely wooded region is where Eric Rudolph, the Atlanta Centennial Bomber, hid out for so many years. Simple conversations to break the ice, and to make everyone more comfortable for the difficult questions I had come to ask and hopefully to get answers. I found Marilyn extremely willing to talk about Jackie, although it was difficult for her at times. She still has guilt feelings about not being there when Jackie desperately needed someone, especially after Jackie had always been there for her.

We spent several days in Ashville and had plenty of time to talk with both Jeff and Marilyn. We were not able to meet their son Ben as he was working in another city and unable to come home during our visit. They also have a daughter, who at the time was in Japan doing an internship for one of her college classes so we missed her also, but we were shown all the photos she had sent home from her trip. She is truly a beautiful young woman. Jeff and Marilyn have every reason to be extremely proud of both of their children and as Marilyn said, "Jackie would be proud also."

Marilyn had been reassigned to the Oak Knoll Naval Hospital in Oakland, California, when she left Japan in August 1979. Occasionally she and Jackie would be able to get together and see each other, but many times their schedules conflicted. Marilyn said the weekend Jackie was murdered she and Jeff had planned to drive to Lemoore to see Jackie, but due to one of their disagreements they decided at the last minute not to go. To this day, Marilyn still feels the guilt for not going, as she feels if she had been there with her, Jackie would not have gone to the Marina alone, and would be alive today.

We asked Marilyn where she was when Jackie was killed and how she heard about it. She said she was at work at the Oak Knoll Naval Hospital when she received a call from Japan and the person said, "Have you heard? Your roommate was killed", but the caller didn't have any other information. Her immediate thought was it was Dee, another corpsman from Japan days, and she picked up the phone to call Jackie and tell her. Before she could complete her call another call came in from NIS wanting to talk to her to see if she knew of anything suspicious or of anyone who wanted to harm Jackie. As soon as she finished talking with NIS she called the base in Lemoore to find out more details, and the person answering the phone wanted to know who she was. When she said "Marilyn Williams", he said, "Oh, she spoke a lot about you", and then had her talk to the Commander who informed her as to what had happened. She had wanted to go to the memorial service held in Lemoore but was unable to go. She then planned to go to Wisconsin for the funeral and her Grandmother passed away and again she missed the services for Jackie. These memories were extremely hard for Marilyn to go through and it was a very emotional Marilyn who told us her story.

Marilyn said the last time she saw Jackie was in September 1980, when Jackie and a friend went to Oakland for the Naval Regional Center softball tournament. After the game they followed Marilyn to her apartment for a short visit to see Ben and then went on their way back to Lemoore. Little did she know that in less than a month Jackie would be gone forever. Marilyn still remembers Jackie as a "very good friend, one who actually helped you through when you were all alone."

When Marilyn left the Navy she went to work for the State of North Carolina, Employment Security Commission where she is now an assistant manager. She has now been with the state for over two decades and her plans are to stay there until she can retire. Marilyn has had another issue to deal with, this time at her workplace, and one which happened just a couple of years ago. On one of her days off, a phone call came in on her line. The person left a voice message, rambling on almost incoherently regarding his claim but did not leave a name or contact number. The next day when Marilyn listened to her messages she tried to determine who the person was, and in talking with a co-worker they thought they had it figured out. The co-worker started making telephone calls trying to locate the person they thought had made the call. At the same time Marilyn started calling another office for information. Suddenly everyone in their office started saying that no one could get through to the other office. All lines were cutoff. Finally one person did get through and the response was a very quick, short sentence that some one had been shot and they thought he was dead, then that line was cutoff. These were all close co-workers talking to each other and panic quickly set in. Who was dead and what had happened?

When everything was finally over and information became clear, it was a very close friend of Marilyn's who had been shot in the head and killed. The disgruntled claimant that had phoned the day before had gone into an office, killed one employee and injured another. Again, Marilyn had another tragic death to deal with and the guilt once again of not being available, this time when the original phone call was made. She blamed herself and felt if she had been at work that day to take the call, calm the person down and determine what he wanted or needed, perhaps no one would have died.

CHAPTER 21
I CAN STILL SEE HER SMILING FACE

In January 2007, I received the following e-mail from Dee Murphy, a fellow corpsman that Marilyn Williams had spoken of. Marilyn has kept in touch with Dee all these years and was the source for my locating Dee. Marilyn had told her of my writing this book and had suggested she contact me as she was also one of Jackie's close friends in both Corps School and in Japan. It did take Dee a while to answer me but her e-mail explains her delay and her feelings.

"Dear Tom,

"Thank you for taking the time to tell me about the book and fill in some details of Jackie's life. It was painful hearing about the details of her death; I think part of me didn't want to know. That may be the reason it took me so long to contact you. It was avoidance. I realize how selfish that is especially considering all the pain Jackie went through. I've written this and many memories over and over again in my mind this past week. Something rather odd, yet special to me, happened last Saturday on our drive to Huntington Beach. It's about an hour and a half drive and most of the way my husband and I talked about Jackie. Mostly I talked, he listened and held my hand at times, I cried, and tried again to make sense of why it happened to her. I wondered, why didn't anyone hear her struggle? Why wasn't anyone around to help? Why, why? Why someone who seemed so cautious and careful, and took so few risks would end up like that? Not that anyone deserves that fate but when I think of all the risks I took (and have taken) especially during those years...it just doesn't make sense. And I don't want to do a disservice to Jackie's memories because my own are so fuzzy. My husband, Steve, was so comforting and said what I know is true. It wasn't her fault and really had nothing to do with her being cautious or not. She was a victim; he, her assailant and murderer did it. He told me don't worry about what you write, just start writing and the memories will come. About an hour into the drive we weren't sure if we could still get the same exit since we had taken the toll road which differed from the Hyatt Hotel's directions. I called the hotel. A lady answered, 'Huntington Beach Hyatt, this is Jackie speaking'. I said, 'Jackie we need directions'. Steve's eyebrows went up and I smiled. Anyway, we were told the toll road would put us on highway 405 so we could again follow the hotel's directions. Steve said, 'So Jackie answered the phone'. It was uncanny. We were at the hotel Saturday thru Monday. I never saw anyone named Jackie working at the front desk the whole time we were there.

"Jackie and I met in Corps School, I don't remember exactly where or when. We got to know each other better in mid August 1977, at Travis Air Force Base, when we were 'bumped' off the military plane that was to take us to Japan. Some

Captain's family got our seats and a few other E-2s' seats that day. We were sent to the barracks at Travis for a couple of days. My memory is a little fuzzy about some details. I remember meeting this guy, Bobby, another 'bumpee', who was on his way to Yokosuka to meet the USS Hammond. I can't remember if he and I and Jackie went to San Francisco to sight-see or if she and I went? But I do remember being at Pier 39 with Jackie at a little Yogurt shop and the Greek owner telling us that Elvis Presley had just died. It was August 16, 1977. The next day we took a civilian plane from San Francisco to Haneda, Japan and a Japanese driver in a black car took us to the Yokosuka Hospital. We had to check into Barracks A because the hospital barracks were full. We roomed with Marilyn and a girl named Bertha at first. Later Marilyn and I roomed together and Jackie and Chris and then later, Jackie and Sallie were bunk mates. Jackie and I worked on Ward 2B together, sometimes the same shift. She was a conscientious, caring and skilled corps person. You knew if you followed her shift, her nursing notes would be complete, thorough and legible. She was very serious about her work. I used to joke with her and call her 'Nurse Wurst'; the implication of Wurst being like 'worse' was funny to everyone including her, because it was so far from the truth. She was one of the best, if not the best corps person on the ward. We went to Korea together sometime in 1977 or early 1978; on a military hop and stayed a few days and did a *lot* of shopping. Jackie was frugal, smart and knew how to find the best deal, even in Korea where everything seemed to be a good deal. I think we both had leather coats made at a tailor shop. There was a midnight curfew on the base in Korea. Korean soldiers stood on the wall with guns prepared to shoot anyone out after midnight. Erring on the cautious side Jackie wanted to make sure we were inside the guest barracks by 7 PM, or by dark. One night I went to the club for a couple of hours, came back at 10:00ish. Jackie had waited up for me and then went to bed minutes after I came in.

"By May 1978, I was staying out on the 'Honcho' in a little house with friends. I hadn't officially moved out of the barracks so I went back and forth to get my things, etc. That's where I was the day Jackie was attacked. A NIS agent knocked and came in, told me what happened and took me to the station, (for lack of a better word) where Jackie was. I marvel at how quickly NIS/NCIS found me. I guess as I look back I'm sure she was in shock. I felt terrible. I didn't know what to do or say. All I could do was hug her again and again and keep asking if she was alright. I think she sensed my inadequacies and tried to smile and say she was alright. She didn't talk very much about it, at least not to me. Soon after that, I moved to that house on the Honcho. I lived there for several months until moving with my friend Ellen to the same apartment building in Kinagasa where Marilyn and Jackie lived. I think we all moved there at the same time along with Dessa and Katie. Many times we visited each other's apartments. Mostly I went to their apartment to visit. Jackie and Marilyn and of course little Ben. Another friend of ours, Adelle, lived in a house nearby and sometimes we went to her house for dinner. Until September 1978 Jackie and I continued to work together on 2B and although we lived in that apartment building we saw less and less of each other. I left Yokosuka in September of 1979.

"I don't remember the last time I saw Jackie. But I can still see her smiling face, the way her eyes squinted and smiled too.

"Tom, thank you for writing a book about Jackie. Thank you for preserving her life and her memories.

Fondly,

Dee Murphy"

Dee later wrote, "Every now and then memories come to mind... Monty Stratton is the one who called me when Jackie was killed. I can't remember if he was still in Japan or in Oakland or where? He broke down on the phone; we cried together and couldn't speak for several minutes. I had to leave work, the Internal Medicine clinic at the Naval Hospital, for the rest of the day. Jackie and I celebrated a birthday together in Japan, her's was July 16, mine July 14th, she was a year older. We celebrated on the 15th in some lounge or barracks lounge in the hospital barracks. Quite a few of our fellow corps people were there. When we lived in Kinagasa I worked part time at the Waterfront restaurant on the base after working days at the hospital so often times didn't get home until later. I usually saw Jackie and Marilyn on the weekends.

"I think I told you that I went Navy Reserve after breaking service for a year, retired as a Chief in 1999. I challenged the state boards and got my LVN license in '81. I worked at plasma centers, Doctor's offices and hospitals, etc. My husband and I moved from San Diego in '83 to Bremerton, Washington and then Norfolk, Virginia finally returned to San Diego, California late '86. I worked for a group of surgeons in El Cajon while pursuing degrees in teaching. I got my BA in Behavioral Sciences before leaving San Diego and then earned my teaching credential and master's in education in '90. I was recalled to active service (Desert Storm) from Aug. '90 to June '91 and finally got a teaching contract in San Diego district in '91. I've taught since then, have taught kinder, 1st, 2nd, 3rd grades and now 5th for two years, and have earned credentials to work with gifted and 2nd language kids of which there are many of the latter. Speak enough Spanish to communicate with parents."

Like all the young Navy people I found that were friends of Jackie's, Dee went on with her life and had a very successful career. Jackie was particular in choosing her friends and she had a way of attracting smart individuals with so much potential, like herself. Today she would be extremely proud of all of them and their accomplishments. I'm sure she is looking down, smiling and nodding her head, "Yes".

CHAPTER 22

FOR CARL IT WAS BITTERSWEET

CDR Carl Tresnak, MSC, U.S. Navy Retired

July 16, 2006, would have been Jackie's fiftieth birthday. On that day Carl Tresnak put on his Navy Commander's Dress Blue uniform and together with his wife, and Don and Phyllis, Jackie's parents, drove the short distance from the Wurst farm to the cemetery. There he alone quietly knelt down by the military gravestone for Jackie, placed the Navy Nursing Staff Corps emblem on the gravestone, and said his final goodbye to her. After a few moments he rose, slowly saluted her, took three crisp, measured steps back, and then walked over to the family. Finally, he had his chance to say goodbye to the young girl he had walked away from over twenty-five years before. The girl that had haunted him all these years as he remembered how deeply in love they were, and how before they could resolve their differences she was so brutally murdered.

The Sun, Osceola, WI, news media article of CDR Carl Tresnak, MSC, U.S. Navy. Photograph by Kyle Weaver

A reporter from *THE SUN* newspaper in Osceola was there to record the moments at the cemetery, and wrote a beautiful article for his paper which included a large photo of Carl saluting Jackie at the grave. He quoted Carl saying, "Jackie had a tremendous effect on everyone she met, she has a tremendous legacy. I didn't want this to be something sad. I don't want her to be remembered as the victim of some crime." Phyllis echoed the sentiment. "It's a mixed emotion," she said. "We feel he'll have his closure."

Donald and Phyllis Wurst at family farm

Carl had always said someday he planned to visit her grave as he felt it necessary to tell her what he had felt all these years. After talking with me these past few months and writing down his memories, he decided it was the right time to make his visit to Osceola, Wisconsin. Don and Phyllis had known Jackie was in love with Carl and also knew of the break-up. This was the reason Phyllis had numerous times in my visit softly suggested I contact Carl. Now the Wurst family again welcomed two strangers into their home in memory of their daughter. Carl and his wife Deanna were treated to the wonderful mid-west hospitality and allowed to see where Jackie grew-up, and how she came by her strong character and high moral values.

Carl and Deanna's visit was short, only a weekend, as they both had obligations at their work places. For Carl it was bittersweet. He told me some time later, after he was able to reveal his private thoughts, he told Jackie when he was kneeling at her grave, "I was sorry for being stupid and a fool and for hurting her." He said, "I told her that I missed her and still loved her to this day." The rest of his private talk will remain with him, private forever.

Chapter 23
Funeral Sermon for Jackie Wurst
(killed Oct. 5, 1980)

After the article of Carl at the gravesite appeared in the local news press, Don and Phyllis began receiving numerous phone calls from friends who once again wished to console them. They received calls from people they hadn't seen in a number of years. One person who called was the former pastor of the church which they attend and who had been the church pastor at the time of Jackie's death. He asked Phyllis for my e-mail address and sent me the following e-mail, which I do quote partially here.

"I was the pastor at Zion Evangelical Lutheran Church during time when Jackie was killed.

"While she was in high school she would baby sit our young children. They would love Jackie's visit because she would always bring children's books along and would read to them. The children loved her.

"I have attached the funeral sermon that I preached at Jackie's funeral.

"In my ministry of 37 years (10 years at Zion) I have officiated at over 200 funerals. The Matthew 10:28 text I used only for Jackie's funeral and never repeated it.

"The experience changed my ministry. It made me more dedicated to bring the comfort of the Gospel to people who have suffered a terrible loss. Our life on earth is so short. The time the Lord gives us as time of Grace is a gift from him. A time to learn about what Jesus has done for all people, even the murderer who was only able to kill the body but not the soul. This time of Grace is a time to come to faith and be assured of the crown of life.

"Sincerely yours

Pastor Roger E. Waller"

He then had the complete funeral sermon attached to the e-mail. I have included a portion of that sermon with Pastor Waller's permission.

"Funeral Service, October 15, 1980

"Dear fellow redeemed, friends in Christ Jesus, our Lord and Savior, But especially you the family of Jackie Wurst. Father, mother, brothers and sisters.

"We now know how Job must have felt when the messengers kept coming and reporting to him the tragic news about the loss of – everything that he had. – first messenger told him, - All oxen & donkeys, and servants with them killed; next sheep and servants killed; next all camels, servants killed, finally he is told, that, ALL his sons and daughters were killed.- One messenger after the next with tragic news for Job, a child of God.

"It has been very similar for you the family these last few days. You received one tragic report after the other. With each report and more details of what happened there was more sorrow and pain and more unanswered questions.

"We hoped against hope that what we were hearing was not true but only a terrible nightmare from which we would awaken and someone would tell us it was all a mistake. But we know now that Jackie is gone, her body is dead and someone has ended her life in a very cruel manner.

"What has happened will be very hard to forget. The feelings that are within us and especially you the family are very hard to express. We feel sorrow, loss, grief and pity for you the family, relatives and all those who knew Jackie. But we as Christians also have feelings for the person or persons, who took Jackie's life, feelings of sorrow, grief, pity.

What happened did not happen without God's permission. But that does not answer the many questions that we have which are all summed up with the question, "Why?" Why did this happen? Job's response to all the tragic reports was not an answer to the question why – but a statement of truth. 'The Lord gave and the Lord has taken away; May the name of the Lord be praised.' (Job 1:21) The Almighty God can use what has happened for our good. May the Holy Spirit guide us as we search for comfort from, the Word's of Jesus: *'Do, not, be afraid of those – who kill the body but cannot kill the soul. –Rather be afraid of the one who can destroy both soul and body in hell.'"*

The Pastor's sermon continued with "what the Lord Jesus would teach us through the crime which has shocked all of us." He went on to consider 3 points. "1) What He would say to the 'criminal ('s) 2) What He would say to the victim 3) What He would say to all of us."

This was a very inspiring and very comforting sermon to the Wurst family at their time of grief. As Pastor Waller said later in a phone call to me, it was a very difficult sermon for him to present and one which he never felt he could use again. He said he would be pleased to have this included in this memory of Jackie Wurst.

CHAPTER 24
"CARL, IT'S OK"

My phone rang and on the other end was a voice both excited and at the same time very emotional. Carl Tresnak said, "Tom, do you know what today is?"

I answered, "Yeah sure, it's October 5ᵗʰ. The anniversary date of Jackie's death."

"Well, you will never guess what came in today's mail. I came home from an exceptionally bad day at work, stopped at my mail box and there was a large, heavy, manila envelope stuffed inside. I looked at the sender address and it read, "Naval Criminal Investigative Service Headquarters, Code 00LJF". I went inside my house, opened the package and a cover letter describes how they had completed processing my request to have Jackie's letters returned. Here are all the letters. Well, actually just photocopies as they kept the originals. The first page is an envelope addressed to "HM3 Carl Tresnak, U.S. Naval Regional Medical Center, Japan" and the return address in the upper left says, "HM3 Wurst, Naval Hospital, Lemoore NAS", the postmark date is 04 Sept 1979."

It took me a moment to understand what Carl was talking about as he was so emotional in describing the packet in his hands. Neither one of us could believe it. What were the chances of those letters arriving on the twenty-sixth anniversary of her death? Carl had asked NIS several times for the return of his love letters and he had been told either they were lost or they had been destroyed or no one knew where they were. I had told him I believed they most likely had been retained as this had been a homicide case. Back in March when he had contacted the NIS Regional Office in Japan it was suggested he request their return under the Freedom of Information Act (FOIA) and if they were still in existence they would be returned within two to three months. It had now been over six months since he had filed for the return of those letters. Now here he was on this specific day with this large packet of letters, and as he later told me, "The writing took on an even greater importance at that very moment. It was as if Jackie herself wanted to have a say and here were her very words."

That night Carl sent me the following e-mail.

"I think I told you once that October has always been an odd time for me. I've always had feelings of emptiness and kind of a dread that cold weather was on the way. This time of the year meant the end of baseball season and that school was really back in session after a great summer, all kind of depressing.

"When Jackie was killed in 1980, the exact time and place and events have forever and indelibly been stamped into my mind, so much so that every October 5th I automatically start to feel that emptiness again.

"This last year (you called me right before Thanksgiving last year if I remember correctly) of remembering Jackie has allowed me to do a little introspection and self assessment of what kind of person I was in 1979-80 and what I am now. I thank you again for all the positive things that have come from this book as *all* of it has been positive in so many ways."

The following day he sent another e-mail---

"06 Oct 06

"I read those letters last night. It was difficult at times to read through my tears. Tears not just of sadness but also of joy. Jackie was so wise at her age. I had forgotten that in her simple way of talking and writing she could distill things down to make sense and she always understood. In those letters she expressed her love for me, her love and respect for people and specifically says in one of her letters that she wasn't sure what her lot in life was. I guess now I know for sure, because that wonderful girl, so long ago, would make a difference to so many people even today. She represented what was good about people and her tragic loss did not diminish the hope that there are people like Jackie that can make such a positive impact on our lives. Her smile and loving, caring nature are not gone from our hearts. We'll always miss her."

Carl and I had several phone conversations and a number of e-mails regarding these letters. For him they brought back many memories of the good times they had together and also the heartache over their break-up. He told me how he still vividly remembers the day she left Japan to return to the United States. She was wearing a green silk sleeveless blouse and he took photos of her and she had "kind of a smile" on her face but her face was in shadows. He said that morning she cried and cried and couldn't stop. He finally told her she had to stop crying so he could take some pictures. He said she didn't look sad in the photos but as soon as he finished taking them she started crying again

After Jackie left Japan she was essentially alone, even in a room full of people and with a smile on her face. He said throughout her letters she would ask if he still missed her and if he was as lonely as she was and generally displayed her insecurity. His letters back to her were very supportive but he said, there was such a delay in the conversation, and he didn't write as often as she did. He said, "When you are there with someone you can ask them what they are feeling or give them assurance and I couldn't do that for Jackie."

Carl also told me seven months passed before they were able to see each other and things had changed during that period of time. He said they didn't talk about the differences they had after she left Japan "so I was stuck in my own thoughts and doubts and couldn't talk to anyone about it either. I guess Jackie and I were in the same boat but I wasn't smart enough or understanding enough or compromising enough to keep the flame burning. Our time in Japan was overwhelmingly happy and like fireworks that burnt so brightly. We were so close and content and growing together and then she was gone. I'm convinced that if she had lived we would have been close again, even if it only had been as friends. I'll never know if she got the final letter I sent her asking her to spend Christmas with me when I got back to the states. I sent that letter about a week before she was killed and her brother David claims that the backpack she was carrying when she was killed had a letter from me in it."

In another e-mail written about a week later, Carl wrote me "I can see now that she was much wiser than me in those days. It's very apparent to me now, reading what she said, that we certainly could have compromised on our differences I just couldn't see it then…..You can also see that she had no ill will toward me, she was hurt but not angry or bitter and that was what made her so special. I have to live with being wrong, and it makes me sad to this day. Jackie got all the bad luck a person could ever handle, but she handled it. It didn't break her spirit but strengthened it. I told her when I was in Wisconsin, kneeling at her grave, I missed her and still loved her to this day. Getting these letters back is her voice saying, 'Carl, it's OK'. I'll always believe that."

Chapter 25
Dear Carl......Love, Jackie

Within just a few days I received a complete set of all of Jackie's letters. Carl felt that by my reading them I would have a better insight into his relationship with Jackie. For me, I knew this was the only voice of Jackie's I would ever hear. All the other thoughts and feelings I had received were from her family and friends. Now I had her own writings to give me an actual understanding of what she thought and felt.

As I read the letters I realized what a difficult time this had been for Jackie, leaving the young man she was deeply in love with, and at the same time moving to a very different environment from any she had known before. Usually the term *cultural shock* is used to explain the differences felt when moving to a foreign country, but Jackie's move back to the United States and to the small town of Lemoore had been a true *cultural shock* for her. The isolation of the area, the need to make a new set of friends, the adjustments required to a new job location, these situations all take time to adapt. The transition from an area where she had true life-long friends and had the excitement of living in a foreign country and learning about a different culture, to an area out in the middle of nowhere that is hot and dusty in the summer and cold and foggy in the winter, that alone can be challenging. This all took its toll on her as she now no longer had the support of her close friends. Although, to listen and read what her co-workers and friends later said about her upbeat personality and friendly smile, you would never know the sadness and loneliness she felt inside. But Jackie's letters do give us that insight into her private thoughts and feelings. She felt so alone.

"31 August 1979

"Hi,

"How are you doing? As lonely as me? Well, I finally made it to Lemoore. I was beginning to wonder, tho! I made my flight okay to San Francisco, I got there at 1 PM and my other flight was scheduled for 5:45 but we left an hour late. I sat in the airport, bored and wishing I was with you (I'm always doing that!) I found a good book to read tho so it wasn't too bad. I gave up on watching TV. I couldn't believe the ridiculous shows! I'm staying in the duty room, because they don't have a room in the Waves barracks here. They better let me move off! I'll have to get a car first. Nothing is walking distance like there! I'm going to close and try to sleep. I've had a headache all day and I'm not in the writing mood. Sorry!

"Love, Jackie"

"20 September 1979

"Hi,

"How are you today? As lonesome as me? My day started out good, went bad and has improved a little this pm. I spent the entire morning mounting EKGs. There were a lot of them!

174

Everything went bad after lunch. I had to deliver supplies, and then order more supplies because they want to spend all their money before the end of the fiscal year. It wouldn't be so bad, but the guy who is supposed to be orienting me has been giving me a really hard time. I can take so much of it and he just goes too far all the time. He really upsets me. I asked to get off ½ hour early today so I could get my insurance. A few people got upset because Thursday is field day, and I'd get out of it. I jumped in my car to go, and nothing happened. I couldn't believe it. I'm just getting so frustrated with everything, I'm ready to quit. Then I think of you and I know I can hang on for awhile longer. Everything just seems to be going wrong for me. Anyway, after a consult, it was decided the culprit of my dead battery was the brake lite switch that was put in yesterday. I took it out and had my car jumped. Hopefully it will start tomorrow and I'll get the battery charged. After all that hassle, I went running. I only did 1 ½ miles tonite. My legs complained too much!

"I don't remember if I told you, they're going to make me get a government license and be ambulance certified or whatever. I told them I didn't want to. They say, you <u>will</u> do it. We'll see. I got a letter from my mom today. She told me how nice the weather is there now. I guess she's been really busy canning and freezing vegetables. She also told me about all the fresh sweet corn they're eating. Remember I told you that's what I thought I'd eat the whole time I was home? I can't believe how pessimistic I am! I'm sure glad you're around! You're about the only thing I'm not pessimistic about! I love you and miss you!

"Love, Jackie"

"29 September 1979

"Hi,

"How are you today? I'm okay, just surviving! It seems like forever since I got a letter from you, but it was only yesterday. We don't get mail on weekends here. Today was an okay one for me for the most part. My first 'free' day in a couple of weeks. I tried to sleep late but I kept thinking of all the things I had to do, so I got up. I did my wash, then took my bike over to the gas station to put air in the tires. While there I asked about the smog check for my car and he said he could do it right away. So I went back and got my car. He okayed it, but wrote that it had a bad engine. I already knew that! Besides, I have the new one in back of my car. Then, I took back the tools the guy was going to use on my car and picked up another part for the engine. On the way back, I got stopped by highway patrol because my car was smoking so much. He was very nice, considering, and just gave me a warning and two weeks to fix it. I knew I would get stopped sooner or later! I'm surprised the base police never stopped me. I don't know why it is smoking; it does have enough oil! I check it every time before I go somewhere.

"We had a big event here today. It sprinkled! I guess it hasn't rained here since April. It got so dark and windy, it was kind of neat. I almost miss the big thunderstorms we always got (at home.) The sky would get really dark or a strange orange color, and it would thunder and lightening and then rain. We always used to stand on the porch and watch it, and then when it was over, us kids would run and play in the puddles. My mom didn't like that but we did! Anyway, back to the present.

"Here I am, all lonely and miserable and missing you tremendously. I guess if we make it past the loneliness, we'll survive. I sometimes wonder if that is possible. I'm trying to be more optimistic about this place, but it's really hard. I guess if I liked it here a little bit more, the loneliness wouldn't be quite so bad. Maybe it will be better once I get past the culture shock stage. They say its 3-4 months. I've got a ways to go! Take care. I love and miss you,

"Love, Jackie"

Jackie's days went by with some days better and some much worse. It seemed to her to take forever to adjust to all the changes required at her new duty station. She and Carl periodically would make arrangements to call each other using the government lines. She would send him a copy of her month's work schedule and he would try and call her during those hours. The calls were supposed to be work related and once the telephone operator discovered they were personal she would disconnect the calls. A very frustrating arrangement for the two young people but neither of them had the money to pay the expensive charges for long distance calls in those days. This was the best they could do even if it was at times just a short minute conversation.

Carl also decided to save enough money to take a commercial flight from Japan to San Francisco in order for them to be together. He would take ten days leave and they would drive around California, do as much sightseeing as possible, but mainly they would be together again. The anticipation of being with Carl after these long months apart was very evident in Jackie's letters, and at times seemed to be the one thing she had to look forward to. Whenever she was able to get away from Lemoore for just a day or two and see a different part of California, she would write Carl how she hoped the two of them could go back to the area so she could show him the beauty she had seen.

In their letters they discussed their individual Navy careers. Jackie told how her enlistment would be up in February 1981 and she emphatically would not reenlist. She asked Carl what places he listed on his Dream Sheet, the reassignment areas of his choice, and was happy with his first two choices of Oakland and San Diego, California. Carl definitely planned to continue his career in the Navy.

Jackie had been plagued with a bad ankle for quite a long time. Marilyn Williams, her roommate in Japan, even remembered her having problems with the ankle while in Japan. In late January 1979 Jackie and a group of friends made a ski trip to Yosemite, and she told Carl how she was paranoid about hurting her ankle since the skis she had rented did not fit properly and the bindings were poor. But in spite of several falls on the slopes she made it with no injuries that day.

Jackie was a wholesome young girl with a very religious background. She had grown up in an environment with strong moral values and she retained these same values when she joined the Navy and left home. Some of the young people she saw on a day to day basis became a bit wild once they left their homes and were out on their own. We know from her letters that Jackie was not comfortable around these people when they were partying too much as she wrote Carl, "Sorry, it just isn't my thing and I don't like it at all. I'm still rather paranoid about being alone anyway, without having weird-acting people around."

In early March 1980 Carl finally arrived in San Francisco and Jackie was there to meet him. Carl has told us of his feelings and actions during their visit and now we can hear from Jackie regarding how she felt.

"19 March 1980

"Hi,

"Anyway, back to us, now that I'm more rational and not so upset. Like I tried to say, but I don't think came out, I do feel the same as you, in the respect that a marriage between us might not have worked out. Mostly because of our different views on religion. So for our different backgrounds, I don't think they're as far apart as you think, especially after meeting your family. To say the least my leave wasn't what I expected it to be. That'll teach me to have too high of expectations. I didn't have all that great of a time, I guess because of your attitude toward me. Like I told you, I felt like you had built a wall around yourself, and you were treating me so cold and impersonally.

"I'm really glad we finally 'cleared the air' and still have our friendship. I'll always wish the best for you, in whatever you do. No hard feelings or accusations! I hope you don't mind me saying all this. I wanted to tell you in person but I was too upset to say what I wanted. I'm still upset, and hurt terribly, but I guess in time I'll find glue to put my shattered heart together.

"Love, Jackie"

Jackie continued to write Carl, although, not as often as before their leave. The tone of her letters changed completely. Before their visit she was trying hard to adjust to her new environment and trying to get herself settled and because of her loneliness her letters were for the most part very short. They mostly stated how lonely she was and the problems she was having. After Carl's visit her letters became much longer and told more of her everyday activities, but they were less personal in their tone. However, she always ended each letter stating how she missed Carl and still loved him, but the emotion was not there like before.

On July 20, 1980 Jackie wrote Carl a long letter telling about her baseball team she played on. She sent him a clipping of the Athlete of the Quarter write-up regarding her and merely commented, "It sounds nice, anyway!" She inquired about his family, talked about her parents having been to California to visit her. She wrote about her co-workers and their problems and then remarked how she only had seven more months left in the Navy and how she would be glad to finally return to the civilian life. Then her tone changed again and she wrote, "I sometimes wonder if life is worth all the hassles (No, I'm not suicidal!) I'm still waiting to find out what my purpose in life is. You're probably thinking I've flipped, too! Not yet, anyway! I guess I spend too much time thinking, without any verbalizing. This is starting to get deep, I better stop! I'm going running as soon as I finish. Maybe that will clear my brain of all its morbid thoughts. I try to run on the days we don't have practice. It's still hot out though, I hope I don't melt! Take care, I miss you.

Love, Jackie"

Was Jackie having a premonition of what was coming in just a few weeks? Did she feel her life was to be cut short at a young age? Did she wonder if people would ever think of her again if something happened to her? From this letter we do get the impression these or similar thoughts went through her mind. Was she trying to tell us she did know what her fate in life was but still wondered what the purpose was?

As an investigator I always wondered why Jackie couldn't run away from her assailant. She could "run like a deer" as more than one person had told me, and she was in good physical condition and had exceptionally strong upper body strength. However, Jackie had a long history of trouble with both of her ankles. Through out the series of letters written during the 1979-80 timeframe she mentioned a number of times when she had sprained an ankle or twisted it. The last letter she wrote to Carl answered one major question we all had.

"28 September 1980

"Hi,

"Life is as exciting as ever here. At least it's still warm and not raining. Friday I went flying with SEA (sea air rescue). We flew over or thru the Sierras, in the Kings Canyon area. It was great and so pretty. I'd love to go hiking thru there. I'm hoping I can go again this winter. Saturday I went bike riding to the local Marina. I still can't run, so I'm trying to find ways of using up my energy........."

Now we know, Jackie had once again hurt her ankle. Then, one week later on October 5th, 1980, Jackie was brutally murdered at the Marina. She was surprised and taken off guard by her attacker. But Jackie knew what was happening; she could see it all in her mind as she had been through this before. And she had vowed it would never happen to her again, she would fight to the end. She had written this in her diary and she had told Carl, "I would never let that happen to me again". With all the strength Jackie had, if she could have broken free from her attacker for only a moment, she could have out run him. If only she had been able to run.

EPILOGUE
"ONE SMILE IS WORTH A THOUSAND WORDS"

This book of memories was written as a tribute to Jackie and to show how deeply this young woman affected many lives. Some she knew closely—family and friends. But Jackie also affected many others she never knew---Navy personnel, Police and Sheriffs, Naval Investigative Service Special Agents; all those who worked so diligently and persistently to locate and bring to justice her killer.

Jackie's death should never have happened. Her killer should not have been on the streets at all. His record clearly shows he was a serial rapist and both the California Courts and the Navy Courts bear the responsibility for allowing him to be free to attack over and over until he finally brutally murdered a young woman. Even then he was able to manipulate the system and receive his sentence to run concurrent with other time he was serving. Hopefully, each time he comes up for parole the Boards will review his complete background, and never release him onto our streets and allow him to start up his rampage again.

I am thankful I was lucky enough to read the newspaper article in 1982, and connect the Navy "AD2" acronym to Jackie's death. In a perfect world we would not have violent crimes like this but as we all know, this world is not perfect. Even so, violence such as this, committed against anyone should not go unpunished. As this case languished in the cold case file, I felt such an obligation as an investigator to find her killer and couldn't let the case go unsolved forever. I am proud I have that streak of perseverance which compelled me to constantly be alert for any information which would lead us to her killer and bring him to justice.

Again I used my perseverance to locate her friends and co-workers twenty-five years after her death. I have had many e-mails and telephone calls from some who knew her during her three years-seven months-twelve days in the U.S. Navy. Some of those responses came quickly and some took a much longer time but they were each one worth all my effort. The memories are still as vivid today as they were when Jackie was alive. Jackie's impact on everyone was a positive one and that is a legacy we all should hope for ourselves.

To Marilyn---Without your response to my letter and without your memories of good times and bad times, I would not have been able to show the depth of Jackie's compassion for her friends. Jackie cared about others, was respectful of them and was supportive in her own way. You have followed that same trait all these years in your continuing contact with Jackie's parents. I am amazed at your total recall of those days in Japan, down to the last detail including colors of clothing purchased. I know putting your story down on paper was extremely difficult for you as some of those were painful memories, ones you had buried years ago. I hope your family will read this and understand the difficulties you experienced at your young age, and be proud of all you have accomplished today. My wife and I thank you again for yours and Jeff's hospitality when we were in Ashville, North Carolina. We had a wonderful time with both of you and enjoy being on your e-mail list and hearing all that is currently happening in your family. We also look forward to visiting with you again, and perhaps next time it will be here in California where we can hopefully be as hospitable as you were.

To Carl---You will never know how much I appreciate you opening up your heart and soul to me. I will forever remember our first conversation and your reaction after all these years when I mentioned the name Jackie Wurst. The shock was very evident and the grief was still as devastating as if it all had occurred recently. Your love for her to this day is very clear when you talk about your lives together during 1979-80. Your ability to articulate your guilt for turning away from her when faced with the long separation required by your military career, and again when you were informed of her death, showed us the true depth of your sorrow and your love for this young woman.

I hope I have done you justice and have shown how Jackie was a wonderful young woman who had a lot to give to the world. She was a victim, we can not deny that, but we do know she did not react like a victim, when she was faced with adversity. Jackie gave so much of herself to all around her, to her family, to her friends, her co-workers, and to her patients. Your memories of her are to be treasured and are worthy of lasting forever.

To Joslyn, Charlene, Faith and David---She was your sister. The one you played with when you were children, the one you did chores with, and the one you looked up to as a big sister. She was raised the same as you with the same set of high morals and values. She was your sister who wanted to follow her older brother Joslyn into the Navy, she wanted a challenge. She was your sister who came home in a most unexpected way, one difficult to comprehend and understand.

My objective here was to show how her friends loved and admired her for who she was and for her compassionate and caring way, both in her Naval Service and in her personal life. As you read about Jackie I hope you were able to see how she did make an impact on all these different lives. I also hope you will understand how those of us who never met Jackie were influenced by what we learned of her in our investigations.

You have told me how you know she watched over your family and was your special angel. Having come to know the Wurst family this past couple of years I do believe that and I also believe she has smiled down on all many times. There is a lot to smile on in this gracious family.

I truly appreciate you sharing your thoughts and feelings and memories with me and I have shared them with your permission. I know it was not easy to go back and remember not only your childhood days, but also those dark days in October 1980. Your thoughts and feelings were important to me and I thank you for all your letters and e-mails.

To Phyllis and Don, Jackie's Mom and Dad---As Jackie's parents you knew she was special. When you received all those cards and letters after her death you then knew she was special to many people. The strong moral values you instilled in her gave her the character which made such an impact on her many friends. Her love, her compassion, her thoughtfulness of others, all came from her wonderful family life. She had been taught these things by the way you both have lived your lives. You were perfect examples to her. You showed your warmth and kindness to my wife and me, total strangers who entered your lives and asked you to open those deep wounds after many years of healing. You also welcomed Carl Tresnak and his wife into your home to help him deal with his grief from so long ago. I can only hope this did not cause you more pain, as it was not my intention.

You shared all your memories with me and I appreciate that from the bottom of my heart. It was important to me to have as much information regarding Jackie as I could obtain, and yours was the most important of all. Without your help I would not have known who her friends were and who in turn helped by adding their thoughts and memories. I am certain portions of these writings were extremely difficult for you to read but they were a part of the story of Jackie. They needed to be told. From there came the true picture of who Jackie was and how she affected many of her closest friends. You can truly be proud of the daughter whose smile is remembered by so many.

And to Jackie---You were here for only a few short years, way to few. You had a bright future ahead of you; you would have made a wonderful Registered Nurse as evidenced by your Navy Corps days. No one's life should be taken the way yours was, but it does happen. Those left behind to grieve had to adjust their lives and accept their loss and try to live without you. Somehow they managed to do so, but they were all left with scars which they did their best to cover. Your sister says she knows you have taken care of them and have smiled down at many times. She feels it in her heart. Many have said you would be embarrassed at any attention addressed to you, and I guess this would be in that category. However, this is written only as a tribute to you and to the way you lived your life. You did impact these and many other people in those few years not only with your graciousness, thoughtfulness and exceptional kindness but also with your beautiful smile. We should all hope to have a legacy such as this. We only ask that you keep smiling on each of us. We remember, "One smile is worth a thousand words".

ACKNOWLEDGMENTS

Jackie Wurst was brutally murdered on October 5, 1980 and since that time I have told many people the story of her life and untimely death. The senseless homicide of this young woman, who served her country with great dignity and pride as a Hospital Corpsman Second Class in the U.S. Navy, caused me to consider writing her story. However, my own career as a Special Agent kept me extremely busy with travel and a heavy work schedule. Finally, after my retirement from NCIS, and after having this story in my head for twenty-five years, I began to locate family and friends of Jackie's and then to write her story.

Most of all I wish to thank the parents of Jackie, Donald and Phyllis Wurst, for their willingness to answer my questions. I know it wasn't easy to bring all those memories to the forefront after these twenty-five years.

I also thank my wonderful wife, Beverly, for her assistance and encouragement to continue to write this book. It is no secret that it would not have happened had it not been for her devotion to me and unwavering support.

Scores of people have helped me in many ways from locating former friends to writing their memories and I wish to thank each of them for all thy have done. Some had more to contribute as they were more involved in Jackie's life but each person was helpful in his or her own way. Without everyone's input I would not have been able to show the true story of Jackie. It would be a long story in itself to tell of the total involvement of everyone who helped this first-time writer in my quest to tell the story of The Relentless Pursuit of the Truth. Therefore, with my sincere thanks for everyone's time, thoughts and memories, I am listing their names in alphabetical order.

Christine Appel, former HM3, U.S. Navy

James A. Ashley, former HM3, U.S. Navy

Pamela Lynn Blizzard

Michael Boston, Captain, U.S. Navy, Retired, and wife Sandi

James Busey, Admiral, U.S. Navy, Retired

Sheriff Tom Clark, Office of the Sheriff, County of Kings

Harvey Dwyer, HMC, U.S. Navy, Retired

Willie Ewing, M.D., former Commander MC, U.S. Navy

Charlene (Wurst) Flotterud

Hanford Sentinel, Hanford, California

Darryl Henry, Captain, Office of the Sheriff, County of Kings, Retired

Special Agent Ronald Jansen, NCIS, Retired

Special Agent Hugh Kimball, NCIS, Retired

Special Agent Robert Kohlmeyer, NCIS, Retired

Special Agent Ralph Lomele, NCIS, Retired

Special Agent J. Brian McKee, Director, NCIS, Retired

Special Agent C.D. Mugglesworth, NCIS, Retired

Dee Murphy, HMC, U.S. Navy, Retired

Faith (Wurst) Niemann

Larry Orth, Detective, Office of the Sheriff, County of Kings

Special Agent Greg Redfern, NCIS, Retired

Special Agent Steve Spears, NCIS, Retired

Special Agent Wendell Taguchi, NCIS, Retired

Carl Tresnak, Commander, MSC, U.S. Navy, Retired

Special Agent James Vorse, NCIS

Pastor Roger E. Waller

Kyle Weaver, *The Sun* newspaper reporter, Osceola, WI

Jeff Williams, former U.S. Navy

Marilyn Williams, former HM3, U.S. Navy

David and Beth Wurst

Joslyn M. Wurst, former EN2, U.S. Navy

Donald Wurst

Phyllis Wurst

ABOUT THE AUTHOR

Author and wife 2007

Tom spent twenty-eight years with the Naval Criminal Investigative Service, NCIS, with overseas assignments for sixteen years in Vietnam, Philippines, Taiwan, Japan, Italy and England. He served as a Special Agent with a specialty of Polygraph Examiner for twenty-five of those years, during which time he earned a legendary reputation. His career in law enforcement has spanned more than forty-five years, and he is currently employed as a Senior Investigator with the Medical Unit of a State Governmental Agency. Tom served in the U.S. Navy attaining the rank of Chief Petty Officer and was later commissioned as a Military Intelligence (MI) Officer with the U.S. Army. His awards include medals from the Japanese Government, the Government of Taiwan, Republic of China, The Vietnam Service Medal, and numerous U.S. Military awards and certificates for outstanding assistance in the resolution of sensitive high level matters. Tom has also received many awards and certificates from State and County agencies for the resolution of criminal matters. Tom is a graduate of St. Mary's College in Moraga, California.

The story of Jackie Wurst is only one of the many homicide cases Tom worked during his career with NCIS. But in this case there were many similarities in both his and Jackie's background; both were from the same state; both with assignments in Japan and northern California during the same timeframe; and both with the same dedication to their respective careers. The more he learned of this compassionate and caring young U.S. Navy Corpsman the more determined he was to solve this horrific crime. As this case became colder and colder he felt compelled to find her killer and bring justice to Jackie and her family. Tom's persistence and constant awareness finally paid off and eventually led to the resolution of this cold case.

Made in the USA
Middletown, DE
31 July 2020

14131930R00125